CHRIST IN THE CHURCH

CHRIST IN THE CHURCH

A VOLUME OF RELIGIOUS ESSAYS

92951

BY

ROBERT HUGH BENSON

AUTHOR OF "THE KING'S ACHIEVEMENT," "THE QUEEN'S
TRAGEDY," "THE CONVENTIONALISTS," "THE
NECROMANCERS," "NONE OTHER GODS."

*BX
1756
.B47*

ST. LOUIS, MO., 1911
PUBLISHED BY B. HERDER
17 SOUTH BROADWAY

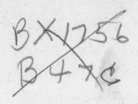

———————

—BECKTOLD—

PRINTING AND BOOK MFG. CO.

ST. LOUIS, MO.

CONTENTS

PART I.— THE THESIS — CHRIST IN THE CHURCH

PART II.— LIFE AND MINISTRY

PART III.— PASSION AND REJECTION

PART IV.— FAILURE AND TRIUMPH

PREFACE

The following chapters have, in substance, been delivered in sermon form in the church of S. Silvestro-in-Capite in Rome, in Lent 1909; in the Carmelite church in Kensington in the Lent of 1910; and in a private house in Boston, U.S.A., in the Eastertide of the same year. I have altered to some slight extent the language used in their oral delivery; but to a large extent I have also allowed that language to stand, as being more appropriate to conferences intended to be persuasive rather than scholastic, and especially in treating of the dramatic scenes of the Passion. It is necessary also to add that the aim of the book as a whole is to be suggestive rather than exhaustive. I am well aware that countless points are not worked out as they deserve, and that it is possible to take exception to many of the arguments. I would only plead in extenuation that the book does not claim to be more than an impressionist sketch, or a sort of table of contents, to serve perhaps some day for the outline of a larger work upon the same subject. It is put forward in the hope that it may suggest a new point of view to some of the many "men of good-will" who only desire to see the truth in order to grasp it. It is not at all meant as a controversial work for those who are determined to find fault with it, or with Catholicism. It is, in short, a well-meant attempt to indicate in a few strokes the wood, as a whole, to those who cannot see it for the trees.

ROBERT HUGH BENSON.

HARE STREET HOUSE: BUNTINGFORD.
November 17, 1910.

PART I

THE THESIS — CHRIST IN THE CHURCH

I

The charge brought most commonly in these days against Christianity in general, and Catholicism in particular, is that it claims in an unique and exclusive degree to contain the whole of truth. Surely, it is said, considering the religious history of the world — the numerous bodies that have flourished in East and West alike, in all the centuries of man's existence — such a claim is arrogant and impossible. We must find the truth, it is said, in the Least Common Multiple of the religious, experiences of all men if we are intellectually democratic; or, if we have aristocratic leanings, in the unanimous conclusions (if any such can be found) of the best independent religious thinkers. Above all, we must be pliant and undogmatic; we must be willing to see the conclusions of this generation overthrown by the next; we must believe in progress even though we are not sure in what direction progress lies. For there is no absolute truth, no final revelation: creeds are no more than forms and symbols of the One Truth as held by various groups of minds and temperaments.

A second charge brought against Catholicism in particular is that it is actually untrue to the spirit of its Founder. Christianity, it is claimed, consisted, in the beginning, of a life founded upon devotion to a Person: Catholicism consists of devotion to a System, to an organized body that is called a Church. The simplest Protestant sect, it is asserted, with its free spirit, its lack of restriction and dogma and ceremony and self-consciousness, and its consequent insistence upon the union of the individual with Jesus Christ, is far more true to the Spirit of the Gospels than is the elaborate organization of the Catholic Church. There is always hope, we are told, in a devotion to a Person; for, as centuries go by, we may perhaps learn to understand the Person better; we may find that He has sympathies — or at any rate that we are capable of attributing to Him sympathies — with the most diverse temperaments, for a Person can be made into a symbol of almost any set of ideas. We may find that Christ is as capable of being interpreted in terms of Lutheran evangelicalism as of Neapolitan fervor; of being treated as the Patron of working men's societies as well as of corrupt monarchies. But there is no hope for worshipers of a dogmatic system, and the less hope as the system is the more elaborate. On all accounts, therefore, Catholicism will not do.

Now in a few unphilosophical pages it is obviously impossible to answer, as they deserve, these extremely deep and far-reaching criticisms; for they go down to the very foundations of all ideas about truth and God. But it will be my object to attempt to answer them rather by a statement of the Catholic position as a whole, than by actually meeting them directly. It will be my endeavor so to describe the life of Catholicism, with certain extraordinary phenomena and coincidences of that life, as to create a presumption at any rate that these two charges are untrue — to point out, in other words, first, that the Catholic Church is productive of results so startling and so unique as to warrant her equally startling and unique claims; and, secondly, that, so far from her having misrepresented the intentions of her Founder, she has actually fulfilled and illustrated them to a degree in which no Protestant body even claims to have attempted their fulfillment. It will not be my intention in these pages to attack even indirectly any positive affirmations of any other religious bodies; for, after all, men are usually more or less right in what they affirm and wrong in what they deny. And it is so great a relief in these days of negation and agnosticism to find any affirmations at all, that no well-meaning person, Catholic or otherwise, will be tempted to do anything except welcome them. Every zealot for truth prefers the affirmations of Mahomet or of Mrs. Eddy to the negations of Sir Oliver Lodge, and the affirmations of Sir Oliver Lodge to the negations of Mrs. Eddy. I shall, then, only attempt to describe a life which I see in the history of the past as well as of the present, so amazing in its beauty, so pregnant of affirmations, so consistent with itself, so steady in its development, and so vital and so undying, as to have at least a right to claim an authority as unique and exclusive as are the phenomena which it produces. And I shall make but one assumption, viz., that the records of the Gospels contain an adequate and accurate transcription of the Life which they portray.

First, it is necessary, however, to give a very brief account of what may be called the orthodox interpretation of those Gospels as held by all Christian bodies in the past. I am not assuming that that interpretation is the right one: it will be my endeavor to create in the following chapters a presumption that it is so. It is first, however, necessary to state it.

II

It has been believed by all Christians up to the present — Christians, that is, in the historical sense of the word — that the Personality of the Figure whom we know as Jesus Christ was the Personality of God; that God sent forth His Son to redeem and teach the world; that this was accomplished by His Life and Death and Resurrection; and that it should be the endeavor of all who call themselves His disciples to imitate the example which He set.

Let us scrutinize that statement a little more closely.

1. It is believed by Christians that this work of Redemption and Revelation was accomplished through Human Nature assumed into union with the Divine — that God did not, so to speak, act merely in virtue of His Deity, but through Humanity as well — that, first a nation, then a tribe, then a family, and then a person, were successively drawn from the world as a whole — Israel, Judah, the line of David, and, finally, Mary — and then, by an unique act of the power of the Holy Ghost, a created substance was produced so perfect and so

pure as to be worthy, in a sense, of becoming the vehicle of the Deity; — this is, in short, the entire summary of the Old Testament — that this substance was then assumed into union with God, and used for His Divine purposes — in short, that the Sacred Humanity of Jesus Christ, by which He lived and suffered and died as man, was the instrument of both Revelation and Redemption; that by a human voice He spoke, that human hands were raised to bless, that a human heart loved and agonized, and that these human hands, heart, and voice — broken, pierced, and silenced as they were — were the heart, hands and voice of Very God. Consider that claim carefully. Though the Person was the Person of God, the nature by which He was accessible and energetic was the nature of man. It is by union with that Humanity that Christians believe themselves redeemed. Thus in that last emphatic act of the life of His Humiliation He took Bread, and cried, not Here is my Essential Self, but " This is my *Body* which is given for you," since that Body was the instrument of Redemption. And, if the Christian claim is to be believed, this act was but a continuation (though in another sense) of that first act known as the Incarnation. He who leaned over the Bread at that " last sad Supper with His own " had, in another but similar manner, leaned over Mary herself with similar words upon His lips. God, according to the Christian belief, used in both actions alike a material substance for His Divine Purpose.

2. Up to this point practically all those known as "orthodox Christians" are more or less agreed, if they will but take the trouble to think out their religion to its roots. And it is at this point also that Catholic Christianity parts company from the rest. For, while Protestants find in the individual Life of Jesus Christ in the Gospels the record of the sum of all His dealings, and in His words "It is finished" a proof that Revelation is concluded and Redemption ended, Catholics believe that there is a sense in which that ending was but a beginning — an inauguration rather than a climax. For, while Protestants hold that there is no vital need of a Church, except so far as a human society is convenient and even necessary for the carrying out and organizing of the energies of individuals, Catholics believe that the Church is in a real sense the Body of Christ, and that in the Church He lives, speaks, and acts as really (though in another sense and under other conditions) as He lived, spoke, and acted in Galilee and Jerusalem. Let me express that under other terms.

We saw just now that all Christians were at one in holding that God assumed into union with Himself at the Incarnation, created Human Nature,

2

in order to accomplish His work — that He took from Mary created substance in which He lived and through which He energized. Very good. Catholics, then, go a step further — a step in a certain sense parallel to, though not identical with, the act of the Incarnation — and believe that He further takes into union with Himself the Human Nature of His disciples, and through the Body thus formed, acts, lives, and speaks. Let us sum it up in one sentence. Catholics believe that as Jesus Christ lived His natural life on earth two thousand years ago in a Body drawn from Mary, so He lives His Mystical Life to-day in a Body drawn from the human race in general — called the Catholic Church — that her words are His, her actions His, her life His (with certain restrictions and exceptions), as surely as were the words, actions, and life recorded in the Gospels: it is for this reason that they give to the Church the assent of their faith, believing that in doing so they are rendering it to God Himself. She is not merely His vicegerent on earth, not merely His representative, not merely even His Bride: in a real sense she is Himself. That in this manner, as well as in another which is not our business at present, He fulfills His promise to be with His disciples all the days, even to the consummation of the world. To express the whole position once more under another aspect, in order to make clear what is the position on which I purpose to enlarge, it may be said that God expressed Himself in terms of a single life in the Gospels, and of a corporate life in the Church.

If, then, we Catholics declare to the Protestant world, you would truly " see Jesus " (as the Greeks in the Gospel), you can see Him only as He really is, living in that Body called the Catholic Church. The written Gospel is the record of a past life; the Church is the living Gospel and record of a present life. Here He "looks through the lattice," visible to all who have eyes; here He reproduces, in century after century and country after country, the events and crises of the life lived in Judæa. Here He works out and fills up, on the canvas of the world's history, that outline laid down two thousand years ago: He is born here, lives, suffers, dies, and eternally rises again on the third day. Jesus Christ is the same yesterday, to-day, and forever.

3. (1) Before passing on to consider the possibility of this position, as well as a very startling analogy supplied to us by recent scientific research, it is suggestive to consider how extraordinarily strong is the support given by the Scriptures to the Catholic claim that the idea which I have described was the idea of Jesus Christ Himself and of His contemporary disciples. It is impossible to dismiss

the claim as one of later growth, as brought about by the ambition of man or the dreams of mediæval mystics, when we reflect upon certain words uttered by our Lord and His Apostles.

For example, the position could hardly be put more explicitly than in the words " I am the Vine, you the branches," or " He that heareth you, heareth Me: he that despiseth you, despiseth Me," or " As My Father sent Me, even so send I you."

For the only distinction possible to draw between the Vine and the branches lies in saying that the Vine stands for the whole and the branches for its parts. The branches are not an imitation of the Vine, or representatives of the Vine; they are not merely attached to it, as candles to a Christmas-tree; they are its expression, its result, and sharers of its life. The two are in the most direct sense identical. The Vine gives unity to the branches, the branches give expression and effectiveness to the energy of the Vine; they are nothing without it; it remains merely a Divine Idea without them. You cannot, that is, apprehend the Vine at all in any real sense *as vine* except through the branches. So, again, in passage after passage of St. Paul's writings, phrases are used that are practically meaningless, or at the best wild and furious exaggerations, unless this identity of Christ and His Church is assumed to have been in the writer's mind. Again and again souls living in union with Christ are named His Body considered as a whole, or as members considered separately; they are said to possess the " Mind of Christ "; they are described in a mysterious phrase, lucid only on the Catholic interpretation, as filling up what is " wanting of the sufferings of Christ "— carrying out, that is to say, on the stage of the world's history, the agony and death recorded in the Gospels, extending before the eyes of the world to-day — and, indeed in every period of history — the bloody sweat, the nails, and the scourge seen in Gethsemane and Calvary. The instruments of the martyr's passion are the instruments of His. It is impossible, I think, for those who at any rate regard the New Testament as an adequate record of the intentions and words of Christ and His friends, to deny that the idea which I have attempted to describe was the idea of the Founder of Christianity as understood by those who heard Him speak.

(2) Now, what has been said up to this point may well be regarded by some critics as being nothing more than a rather forced and metaphorical statement of what is really an impossible position to maintain literally — a presentation, possibly rather picturesque, but hopelessly idealistic, of a mere illustration. I mean, however, a great deal more than that.

It is asked, In what sense can this position be more than a metaphor? A "life," it is said, is a single unit — the life of a plant, of a man, of even the most divinely inspired Teacher that ever lived, is no more than a single life. It is an extension and a stretching of words beyond their proper meaning to say that the Life of Jesus Christ can be identical in any real sense of the words with the corporate life of a multitude of disciples, however deep may be their sympathy with their Master, or however identical their aims and ideals with His.

Now, I would ask those who feel that the criticism just stated is their own, to consider a fact of what is known as organic life, as revealed to us by recent research. Fifty or even twenty years ago, the illustration would have been impossible; at the present day it is a commonplace of science that organic life, however mysterious its unity may be, is, so far as we know it on the physical side, the result of an innumerable company of cells, each possessing an individuality, yet an individuality merged in and transcended, yet not destroyed, by the unity of the body of which each is part. Let us state it in simpler words.

Every organic body — the body, let us say, of a man or a dog — may be regarded under two aspects. First, it possesses its one single and unique life, that may properly be called the life of the body, beginning before birth and ending at that moment called death. Yet, sheltering, so to speak, under this unity — in fact contributing to it — are lives whose number is beyond computation — viz.: the lives of the innumerable "cells" that compose the body. Those cells are continually coming into being, living each its life, and finally dying and passing away with the destruction of the tissues, yet in no sense interrupting by these changes the one continuous life of the body as a whole. The body of a full-grown man has no single cell, at any given moment, which it possessed at the time of his birth; yet his body, we say, has lived continuously from his birth up to that given moment. The cells are indeed individuals, but they are a great deal more, in virtue of their mystical cohesion.

An illustration of this is found in the phenomena of dissolution. The man, as we say, "dies"— his life is extinct — that is, the unity of his life is gone. Yet for a considerable period after that moment the cells still live, each its own individual life. Death marks the destruction of the one body; corruption, of the myriad cells. So markedly clear is this distinction between the two sets of lives in every organic body, that there are actually various terms in use, describing the death of each. "Legal death" is a phrase used for the ordinary extinction of life; "somatic death" for the further event of the dissolution of the individual cells themselves. Or consider the same idea from another point of view. It was commonly held until recently that when the body was wounded or injured, by some mysterious and almost mechanical process, the tissues tended simply to heal themselves. We know now that the blood is full of a countless multitude of units, each with its own life — at least so long as the body lives — its own instincts, its own independent movements, and that when a wound is received, or poison absorbed, it is by an apparently instinctive, yet almost intelligent, process of summoning the garrison or police force supplied by these units that the injury is repaired. Certainly the body is one, it possesses one life and no more; yet it is, simultaneously, a commonwealth of inconceivable intricacy, governed as a whole by one will, yet possessing departments of energy and activity that seem to work practically independently of that will, and yet are subject to it in manners of which psychology and biology can tell us very little. The mysteries of the quasi-mechanical theory are dispelled, but the mysteries of animal life indefinitely increased.

Now this physical illustration may perhaps appear a little forced; yet surely the analogy is too remarkable to be passed over. We considered just now whether it was possible to speak of the Life of

the Church as identical with the Life of Christ —
of the identity, that is, of the myriad consciousnesses
of Catholic Christians with that Divine consciousness of Christ; and we see that recent research supplies us with a parallel, exact, so far as we have
considered it, with the entire Catholic claim on the
point. We see how it is not only possible, but essential, for an organic body — that is, for the highest form of physical life with which we are acquainted — that it should consist from one point
of view of a myriad infinitesimal lives that lose
themselves, and yet save themselves, in the unity
of the whole, and that the unity of the whole, while
it transcends the sum of the individual cell-lives,
is at once dependent on them and apart. If this is
true of physical life, literally and actually, it is
surely not unreasonable to expect that it should be
true also of spiritual life; and the coincidence is
the more remarkable when we remember that the
science of cell-life is of very recent date.

4. It is possible now to contrast vividly the Protestant and Catholic ideas, respectively, of Christianity.

To the Protestant, Christianity consists in the
union of the individual with Christ — of individual
with individual — that, and no more. A Divine
Person, he asserts, lived on earth two thousand
years ago, performed actions, spoke words, finished

His work, and went back whence He came; and true Religion consists in the adherence of the human unit to the Divine Person, with no priest, prelate, church or sacrament, since none are necessary.[1]

Now, the Catholic idea is far larger, as it seems to me, and also simultaneously far more simple, as well as far more elaborate, than the Protestant. For the Catholic, Jesus Christ still lives upon earth as surely, though in another and what must be called a " mystical " sense, as He lived two thousand years ago. For He has a Body in which He lives, a Voice with which He speaks. As two thousand years ago He assumed one kind of Body by which to accomplish His purposes, so He has assumed now another kind of Body in which to continue them; and that Body consists of an unity of myriad

[1] I am aware that some branches of non-Catholic Christianity — notably among the Anglicans — repudiate altogether this individualism in religion. They, too, claim to adhere through the living Church to Christ, and to be members of that Mystical Body in which He dwells. But I am not here concerned with that claim, though personally I do not believe it. It is not my object, as I have already said, to attack in any way other religious bodies, least of all those who hold so much of Christianity in common with Catholic Christendom. It appears to me, as well as to practically all the rest of both Catholic and Protestant Christendom, that the claim is an impossible one, and that it has not the logicality of either side; but I do not propose to discuss this. It is possible that later on in these lectures a good deal that I have to say will indirectly militate against the Anglican position; but I am concerned here only with the two clear-cut conceptions of Christianity as they have always existed amongst us from the Reformation down to the Tractarian movement — the Catholic and the Individualistic.

cells — each cell a living soul complete in itself — transcending the sum of the cells and yet expressing itself through them. Christianity, then, to the Catholic is not merely an individual matter — though it is that also, as surely as the cell has individual relations with the main life of the body. But it is far more: it is corporate and transcendent. The Catholic does not merely as a self-contained unit suck out grace through this or that sacramental channel; the priest to him is not just a vicegerent who represents or may misrepresent his Master; a spiritual life is not merely an individual existence on a spiritual plane. But to the Catholic all things are expanded, enlarged, and supernaturalized by an amazing fact: He is not merely an imitator of Christ, or a disciple of Christ, not merely even a lover of Christ; but he is actually a cell of that very Body which is Christ's, and his life in Christ is, as a matter of fact, so far more real and significant than his individual existence, that he is able to take upon his lips without exaggeration or metaphor the words of St. Paul — " I live — yet it is no longer I that live; it is Christ that liveth in me "; he is able to appreciate as no separatist in religion can appreciate that saying of Christ Himself, that unless a man lose his life, he cannot save it. Still, to the eyes of the Catholic, there moves on earth that amazing Figure whose mere painted portrait in the

Gospels has driven men — artists, seers, and philanthropists — mad with love and longing — and he is part of it. There still sounds on the air the very voice that comforted the Magdalene and pardoned the thief: the same Divine energy that healed the sick and raised the dead is still active on earth, not transmitted merely from some Majesty on high, but working now, as then, through a Human Nature that may be touched and felt. If the Catholic be mistaken in this astounding vision, yet at least he cannot be accused of substituting a system for a Person, since it is the groundwork of his whole life and hope that what men call a system *is* a Person, far more accessible, more real and more effective than one can be who is thought to reign merely in a distant heaven, and no longer in any real sense to be present on earth. The true minister of every sacrament, for example, as every Catholic believes, is none else than the supreme and Eternal High Priest Himself.

This is an amazing claim. It remains now to consider some conclusions that will follow from it if it can be accepted as a working hypothesis.

III

We described in the last chapter the claim of the Catholic Church to be the mystical Body of Christ in which He lives, speaks, and acts. We have not yet advanced any arguments, beyond a few suggestive sentences of Scripture and a physical analogy or two, in defense of that claim (the time for that will come later); we have merely stated the position. But before passing on to these arguments it will be illuminating to notice how two or three further claims made by the Catholic Church, and usually considered as obstacles to her acceptance by the world, are, as a matter of fact, inevitable consequences of her fundamental position.

1. It is perfectly plain that if the Catholic claim to possess Christ in what may be called His " Church Body " be accepted hypothetically, exactly the same authority must be predicated of the voice of the Church as of the Voice of Christ. (I do not mean by this that Catholics hold that the Church is capable of giving new truths to the world unknown to the Apostles; only that in declaring authoritatively what was that Revelation originally given

by Christ, she is as unerring as was He.) This is nothing else than that supreme stumbling-block which Protestants know as the doctrine of the Church's infallibility. Now from the Protestant standpoint the doctrine of Infallibility is, rightly, absurd and even blasphemous. Granted their premisses, their syllogism is perfectly sound. All men are liable to error; the Church consists of mere men; therefore the Church is liable to error. But on the Catholic premisses, Infallibility is simply inevitably and obviously true; for if it be granted that the cohesion of men in the Catholic Church ascends into and is met and transcended by a higher personality, like a cohesion of cells in an organic body, and that higher personality a Divine and infallible one, it follows that the decision of that organic body is the decision of infallible God. If infallibility be predicated of Jesus Christ, it must be predicated of Him in His Mystical as well as in His Natural Body.

That such a transcension of the sum of component cells is possible — that is to say, that the judgment of a number of persons acting in concert is universally recognized as being at least of more value than the mere sum of their votes — this fact is illustrated by the jury system in use in most civilized countries. We give without hesitation to twelve men acting in concert a power over life and death which we would not willingly give to any one of the men taken by himself. It is true that we do not attribute to a jury actual infallibility, since we have no reason for believing that their united judgment has a promise of being ratified and safeguarded by a higher tribunal than that of human opinion, though we believe that that method of decision arrives as nearly to perfection as is possible to obtain; but, *ex hypothesi,* Catholics believe that the consent of the Church does rise to that higher plane — that the sum of Catholic opinion as expressed, let us say, through a Council, does actually rise to a superhuman level of consciousness, that the sum of the human cells mounts up, as in an organic body, to a new unity of life, and that that life is identified and united with a Divine One. "He that heareth you, heareth Me. . . . As my Father hath sent Me, even so send I you." "I am the Vine: you the branches." Infallibility, then, on the Catholic hypothesis is inevitably an endowment of that Body in which there thinks and speaks the Mind of God. *If there be such a Body it must be infallible.*

2. A second point illustrated by this belief is the extraordinary importance attached by Catholics to actual external membership in this Society. It is perfectly true — and we are not in the least ashamed of it — that we will compass the whole world to

make one proselyte; it is true also that we regard
with the most extreme horror those unhappy persons
who once members of the Church are no longer so.

To the Protestant, of course, such an attitude of
mind is inconceivable; for the Protestant, properly
so-called, has no idea that a human society can be
anything besides human. The Protestant may
think that this or that communion is better than the
rest; he may desire his friends to belong to that
which he considers best; he may regret it when they
leave it. But to the Protestant there is not anywhere on earth a society other than human — a
religious club or school, that is to say, to which
it is advantageous or disadvantageous to belong.
He regards therefore the Catholic who will not sit
down at table with an apostate, or the convert who
by his conversion ruins the peace of his family,
as an inhuman monster who sets a greater value
on his own opinions than on the most sacred ties
of blood or charity. And from his own point of
view, upon his own premises, the Protestant is perfectly right.

But to the Catholic who sees in the Church a
human society (often terribly human), but also a
Body in which God dwells, an organism composed
of countless individual cells, but indwelt by a Divine Personality — a Catholic who believes that this
Society is actually redemptive of the human race,

as well as the actually Divine Teacher — more than a school of thought, more than the best religious club in existence, more than the Ambassador of God, more than the Bride of Christ — to the Catholic who believes that the Church is not one among ten thousand, but One, unique, singular and final, between whom and other religious bodies there is no more comparison than between the creature and the Creator — to him, membership in that body, the position of a cell in that organism, is the one thing to which no other can be preferred; and the loss of that membership the one supreme catastrophe or crime. Certainly the Catholic holds that it is possible to belong to the Soul of the Church without external membership in the Body; it is possible, where there is no fault on the individual's side, that he may be united inwardly to the Person who inhabits that body; but such is not God's primary intention, and to forsake the Body is to forsake the soul. In any case the individual loses enormously by being forced to stand alone, · without that grace and strength of unity which external membership in the external body can alone confer.

3. A third point we must notice is the following: On the Catholic hypothesis we have present upon earth in the Catholic Church that same personality and energy as lived upon the earth two thousand years ago in the Figure of Jesus Christ. And we

3

have the same environment — namely, the human nature of the world, human ambitions, interests, virtues, vices, circumstances, strengths and weaknesses, now as then. We should expect to find then, if the Catholic hypothesis is true, the same results now as then. So far as Jesus Christ was accepted or rejected then by the world into which He came, so will He be accepted and rejected now, and by the same kind of people for the same kind of reasons. It resembles the repetition of a chemical experiment. If there is brought to bear under certain circumstances upon certain elements a particular force, the same results will always be obtained. It will be a proof of the identity of the force that, given the same conditions, the same result is so produced. If, then, we find in the history of the Catholic Church the same psychological situations as those recorded in the Gospels continually reproduced under similar circumstances — if we find, that is, Peters and Judases and Pilates swarming round the Church's progress through the ages — if we find that the same comments are made, the same paradoxes generated, the same accusations leveled, the same criticisms, the same bursts of flame and thunder — if we find the lepers healed, the dead raised, the devils cast out, and the same explanations offered of these phenomena by the incredulous — if we find the same amazing claims uttered to the world, and the same repudiations, demurrings, and acceptances of those claims — if, in short, we find that in the Catholic Church, and the Catholic Church only, the endless intricacies and phenomena recorded in the Gospels reproduced on the stage of human history, the conclusion will be practically inevitable that the same Personality that produced those phenomena then is reproducing them now; and that the Catholic claim to possess Jesus Christ in a unique manner in herself is not unwarranted. If the circumstances are the same and the phenomena are the same, the force must be the same.

A further point must also be noticed in this connection.

There are certain arguments drawn from the Gospels in defense of the Divinity of Christ; for example, the story of the Resurrection. Now, if the narrative of the Resurrection could once be accepted as literally true, as it is there recorded, I imagine that very few persons would be found to deny the Deity of Christ. But it is exactly the apparent impossibility of proving that the narrative is true which holds many minds back from the acceptance of the full Christian position. " That is all very well "— says such a man —" but how can I be certified that He did rise again? It was a credulous age, full of expectation of the marvelous. Those who are reported to have seen Christ risen are not

altogether satisfactory witnesses; there are at least
superficial discrepancies in the Four Gospels; further, there are innumerable difficulties of Biblical
criticisms. I am not, therefore, prepared to stake
my whole existence on a doctrine which I cannot possibly verify. He may have risen; He may not have
risen. I was not there, and I did not see it. On
the whole, however, it seems to me more likely that
the Evangelists deceived or were deceived, than that
Christ was very God. Both alternatives are perhaps unlikely; but I prefer that which seems to me
the less unlikely of the two." So, too, with other
similar arguments drawn from the Gospels in defense of Christ's Divinity.

Now the method I propose to follow in these
pages meets, I think, at any rate indirectly, the difficulties of such a critic. It is true that I cannot
demonstrate to the senses the physical Resurrection
of Jesus Christ; but if it were possible to show that
the phenomenon of Resurrection is characteristic
of Catholicism; that Jesus Christ does, not once or
twice, but repeatedly, rise again in the Catholic
Church, rolling away stones far greater than that
which lay on His sepulcher in the garden — if it
were possible to see Him passing through doors
more tightly closed than those of the upper room;
coming through gardens in the dawnlight to lover
after lover — if, in a word, this "sign of the

Prophet Jonas " were a sign of Catholicism everywhere and always, it would create the strongest
possible presumption that the Gospel narrative was
nothing less than sober fact. And if, in addition to
this, it were possible to show that all those other
symptoms of His Divinity recorded in the Gospels
were present in Catholicism — if His progress
through the ages were seen to be accompanied by
bursting tombs, opening eyes, the feeding of multitudes, and, above all, that strange aroma of Divinity
attributed to Him then, the argument would be
vastly increased in significance. Somewhat parallel to this is the observation made by Mr. Mallock
in one of his books. " I can understand," he says,
in effect (though he is not a Christian), " I can
understand the Catholic claim, though I cannot understand any other. The Church says to her children, you must believe these things because I tell
you that I witnessed them myself, and you know that
I am trustworthy. I do not refer you merely to
written books, but to my continuous consciousness
that is called Tradition. You can believe the Resurrection securely because I was there and saw it. I
saw, with my own eyes, the stone rolled away; I
saw the Lord of Life come out; I went with the
Maries to the tomb; I heard the footsteps on the
garden path; I saw, through eyes blind with tears
but clear with love, Him whom my companion

thought to be the Gardener." This, says Mr. Mallock, is at any rate an intelligible and reasonable claim.[1]

Now this, more or less, is an illustration of the way I am attempting to argue. I am not referring simply back to written records, even though personally I may believe those records to be utterly trustworthy; but it is my hope to present, so to speak, the Catholic Church as I know her myself, that you may examine her for yourself. It is my hope to draw attention to what may be called a " personage " now living upon earth whose consciousness runs back for two thousand years, one who has certain characteristics, instincts, and methods that are among her best credentials. And it is my further hope that, comparing what you can see of her with the written papers she holds in her hands, you may identify her for what she really is, and see in the persistence of that character for so long, as well as in her other credentials, at least a strong presumption that she is as unique as she claims to be; and that no hypothesis, except her actual Divinity, will adequately explain the phenomena of her life. In this manner, too, it is possible to fill up even what appear lacunæ to some minds in the writ-

[1] Cf. the whole argument of *Doctrine and Doctrinal Disruption* (Mallock).

ten record. If you have two old MSS., and find that where they are legible they agree perfectly, you are tolerably safe in filling up the illegibilities of one from the clear writing of the other. If you find that in numerous points the Living Church reproduces perfectly the clear testimony of the Gospels, you are justified in accepting the witness of the Church on further points in which the Gospel appears to you doubtful or difficult.

4. Finally, let it be observed that in Catholic Christianity alone is such a claim even made as that which has been described. It may be said, without the possibility of contradiction, that in not one of the great world-religions, in not one of the smallest and most arrogant sects, has the proclamation ever been made that the Founder lives a mystical but absolutely real life in a Body composed of His followers. There have been mystical phrases used occasionally, in certain forms of Buddhism, for example, faintly suggestive of this presence of a Master with His disciples in a very intimate and transcendent manner; but never has it been asserted, in Buddhism, Mohammedanism, Confucianism, in any form of Protestantism, in any savage creed, that the great bulk of the faithful compose a living organism whose dominating personality is Divine. Never, except in Catholic Christianity, has the as-

sertion been solemnly made and deliberately acted upon —" I am the Vine — you the branches "; " He that heareth you, heareth Me."

It is sufficiently remarkable that the Catholic claim is an unique one. " I have read," says St. Augustine, " all the sages of the world; and not one of them dares to say ' Come unto Me.' " I have looked, the Catholic may say to-day, upon all the Churches of the world, all the world-religions, and all the sects, and not one of them dares to take upon her lips the words of very Deity. Many say, " I possess the truth, I teach the way, and I promise the life "; but not one, " I am the Way, the Truth, and the Life." None, except one, and that the Catholic Church, claims to be actually Divine and to utter the Voice of God. The Anglicans dare not excommunicate for heresy; the Nonconformists do not wish to; the Oriental Christians out of communion with the Holy See, though they utter brave words, yet do not exhibit by proselytism and missionary enterprise that confident self-consciousness which Divinity must always show. There is but one body in the world, and that the Catholic Church, which behaves, moves, and speaks as only a Society conscious of Divinity can behave, move, and speak.

But the significance of the uniqueness of this claim is multiplied an hundredfold if in any way it can be justified. If it can but be shown that the claim is a Catholic commonplace, that all the Church's actions are based upon that supposition, that the success of her policy depends upon it, that the unique phenomena of her life spring from it, that, in fact, the very heart of her life is the very assertion itself; if, finally, that assertion made by her, and made by Jesus Christ in the Gospels, produces the same results, and those results impossible of production on any other hypothesis, then, so far as moral proof can go, the claim is vindicated. If, in short, Jesus Christ has succeeded in producing such a Society as this, giving her a confidence that is more than human, and a success unparalleled in human history — if He is able to present to the doubter such a Body as this in which He lives, able to extend hands and side to the touch of skepticism, in proof that it is indeed Himself, risen again and again from what is more final even than death to all merely human energies, then it is hardly possible to imagine any other response but that which Thomas made — "My Lord and my God."

For the appeal of the Church is in its essence an extraordinarily simple and direct one. Certainly it is possible to state that appeal in elaborate and intricate terms, to describe, justify, and indicate by illustrations, metaphors, and the rest, until the case seems too utterly complicated to be true. Yet the appeal itself is as simple as that of a mother to a child. I believe there are very learned books written on the motherly and filial instincts; it is possible to describe a smile in terms of muscles and sinews, and to analyze tears into lime and hydrogen and other elements; yet for all that smiles and tears are the simplest things we know. And the appeal of this intricate Society, claiming to possess as she does the wisdom of the Eternal and the Source of all love, is for all that as direct and as simple as the glance of a woman's eyes into the eyes of her child. All the eloquence of her orators and the learning of her divines, and the elaborateness of her worship, may be summed up in that single sentence that can only adequately be pronounced by the lips of Divinity —" Come unto Me."

IV

Let us now, as these are merely introductory chapters, and therefore rather incoherent and broken up, consider one more preliminary necessary to all accurate thinking — a consideration of what may be called, Points of View.

I am quite aware that to many, especially to those brought up in Protestantism of the more Evangelical type, and still more to those educated under Unitarian or rationalistic influences, the whole point of view which I have attempted to describe, and which I shall hope to illustrate during the following chapters, must seem unreal and fantastic. We live in what is known as a " scientific age "— an age, that is, in which men's minds are inclined to regard as unproven all theses which cannot be reduced to physical formulæ. Let me suggest an example or two of what I mean — in a parabolic form.

Once upon a time three men went to look at a mountain — a geologist, an agriculturist, and an artist. The geologist noticed the formation of the rocks, the strata, and the watercourses; the agriculturist examined the soil, the aspect, and the climate;

the artist sketched the outline, the colors, and the atmosphere. Now, each of the three believed that he had made an exhaustive study of the mountain; each was firmly convinced that he had noted all that was worth noting, and that unless the phenomena of the mountain were reduced to his own terms, they were useless and negligible. Each would have dismissed as an unpractical dreamer his two companions. The geologist would have condemned the agriculturist as sordid, and the artist as a sentimental fool. The agriculturist would have condemned the geologist as a dreamy scientist, and the artist as a trifler. The artist would have dismissed the geologist and the agriculturist as a pair of gross materialists. Yet it is perfectly obvious to ourselves — as laymen in all these matters — that each was right, as I have remarked before, in his affirmations and wrong in his negations. Their evidences were not in the least mutually contradictory, though it may be that they were agreed upon nothing except the existence of the mountain and the testimony of their own senses. Further, it is obvious, that to possess a really adequate knowledge of the mountain as a whole, one must take into account the evidence of all three witnesses; one must know its geological, its agricultural, and its artistic characteristics if one is to arrive at any solidity of truth with regard to the mountain — if, that is to say, one is to be more than merely superficial in one's acquaintance with it.

My parable is not difficult of interpretation.

There stands in the world a mountain — called by Catholics, at least, the Mountain of God — the city built upon a Hill; and it is surrounded by observers.

To one it is interesting as a vast human society, vaster in its range and outline than any similar Society; it is formed on certain lines; it bears the marks of large elemental forces upon its sides; it is constructed in a certain manner; it exhibits certain characteristics; it is, largely, what it is, through purely human and social circumstances. This is the view formed by the historian.

To another it is a society productive of certain results; its soil is capable of bearing some fruits and not others; it has an effect upon the surrounding country; it is capable of development or deterioration. So judges the sociologist.

And to a third it has another aspect. It stands for a certain dominating idea; it has a beauty entirely its own; even more, it conveys to this onlooker an emotion, and even actual knowledge; it reveals facts and relations that are the inspiration of his life. So speaks the student of devotion.

And so the aspects may be multiplied indefinitely. Now the tendency of the age in which we live is to judge one aspect only as worthy of consideration, to reduce the phenomena of Catholicism, and, indeed, of all religion, to one set of formulæ, and to assume that all phenomena that cannot be so reduced are simply negligible. This is surely as narrow-minded and one-sided as to accept the geologist, or the artist, or the agriculturist, as the single trustworthy witness, and to dismiss the rest.

It is simply amazing to observe the complacent blindness of some who are named "modern thinkers," more particularly those who give themselves that name. It is perfectly true that they have contributed enormously to the sum of knowledge that we possess; they have told us innumerable facts in the science of comparative Religion of which we had hitherto known nothing. No Catholic who has any intelligence at all would dream of dismissing "modern thought" as useless or, in its affirmations at least, as misleading; and yet that very Modern Thought which prides itself upon its broadness, its powers of generalization and correlation, has fallen headlong at least as deeply as any mediæval monk, into the delusion that no point of view is of value except its own, no phenomena of any importance except such as can be reduced to its own terms. You have not given an exhaustive account of a Cathedral when you have said that it is built of Bath stone in the decorated Gothic manner, any more than when you have said that it is a place where men worship God, or a place where polyphonic music is performed, or where a Bishop has his seat. All the facts are equally true, and until you are aware of them all you do not know what a Cathedral is.

Now, in the thesis of these chapters I am purposing to treat of the Catholic Church from an aspect familiar to Catholics, and yet one that, it would seem, is almost entirely unknown to non-Catholics. One can find, in book after book, the most admirable treatises upon the Church as a human Society, as a worshiping Society, as a patroness and inspirer of art, as a form of pious Freemasonry, as a police force to keep the poor quiet, as a refuge for the ineffective, as the home of learning. Yet non-Catholics, as a rule, seem simply unaware that there is another point of view, infinitely more significant — whether true or not — from which that Society is regarded as the Body in which the Divine Being tabernacles among men; and that, in spite of the fact, that without this aspect, without at any rate the fact of this belief existing, the main phenomena of that Society's history are inexplicable. This is as wildly unscientific as to think that you have accounted for a Cathedral, if you leave out the worshipers' belief in God. It is no explanation of the Cathe-

dral to discourse about the Bishops, and the word
Cathedra as signifying his seat. A more fundamental point is, Why should there be such a phenomenon as a Bishop at all? Polyphonic music
may be characteristic of a Cathedral; but why
should anyone take the trouble to sing? The architecture may be excellently Gothic; but why is there
such a thing as architecture? Such commentators
as these, on the subject of the Catholic Church,
state, blandly, that she is the best organized Society
upon earth; the most elaborate and august in her
worship; the Mother of the noblest art; the most
exclusive Society in one sense, and the most inclu-
sive in another. Or, again, they denounce her as
the masterpiece of Satan, or the monument of the
keenest human ambitions; or the unhappy result
of an elaborate series of social conditions; or as a
fetish whose sanctity rests upon nothing but superstition or association or circumstance; and they
seem even to be unaware that countless minds as
shrewd as their own have, after an examination
of the evidence all round, deliberately come to the
conclusion that she is actually the Temple of God,
actually the social, corporate, and human Body in
whom the Son of God to-day dwells and speaks,
and that it is for this reason, beneath all the
others, that she is what she is. I am not com-
plaining of their affirmations; I have no quarrel

whatever with the lights they have thrown upon her history — even upon the less reputable parts of that history — her sins of omission or commission, considered as a result of her extremely human humanity — I only protest against their ignorance of the fact that there is another point of view — their tacit assumption that phenomena which do not fall under their categories are not phenomena, and that any account given of her must be unreal and negligible, for the reason that it is in other terms than their own.

This, then, is my object in these papers, to speak of the Church on the hypothesis that she is the Body of Christ in very truth, that what she, as an organism, and not merely as a conglomeration of fallible and faulty units, does, says and lives, is the action, speech, and life of Jesus Christ. If I am able to show a strong presumption that this is so — that the Life recorded in the Gospels is reproduced with inimitable fidelity in the life of the Church, and that the characteristics of that life are the characteristics of a Divine Life, I shall also have established a presumption that she is indeed what she claims to be — the one and unique organ of Divine Revelation. It is necessary therefore to keep this point of view in mind, at least as an hypothesis, throughout. Alexander VI may have been a very wicked man; that does not affect the argument. Catholics may, very often, be very stupid and unspiritual; that does not affect the argument. Transubstantiation may be a very difficult doctrine; it may appear to some that the worship of Mary, as they understand it, is degrading, or the practice of confession humiliating; there may be excellent explanations for the miracles of Lourdes, or the ecstasies of St. Teresa, or the predominance of the City of Rome — all this does not affect the argument in the very least. It is necessary to remember that all these things may seem facts, and yet the Church may be the Body of Christ, and He its Soul and its Supreme Life. Sins of omission and commission on the part of Catholics, stupidities, misunderstandings, apostasies, ignoble and unfashionable circumstances, countless failures, tragedies, comedies and even screaming farces — these simply do not touch the matter at all. Our Lord was betrayed by one Apostle, repudiated by another, and forsaken by the rest; He was the fool of Pilate's court, the butt and buffoon of Herod's. Even when He lived on the earth in the days of his Flesh, " His visage was more marred than any man's, and His countenance more than the sons of men."

PART II
LIFE AND MINISTRY

I

"SHEPHERDS AND KINGS"

We have considered in previous chapters the Catholic claim that the same Character that is portrayed in the Gospel is the Character at work in her own organism — that the Eternal Word of God who united Human Nature to Himself, and, through that Human Nature, as through an instrument, taught and redeemed the world, unites Human Nature still to Himself, and through that Body that is called the Catholic Church still teaches and redeems mankind. We have to consider now what proofs there are of this astounding claim — and, in particular, what may be called the psychological symptoms of His Presence as recorded in the Gospels and as reproduced in the Church. If we find that the identity is practically inexplicable on any other hypothesis, we may take it as at least strongly indicated that the claim is a just one; if, further, we find that such effects are eminently characteristic of what may be expected of the Divine action, we are thereby impelled to suspect that the Character at work is Divine.

1. I propose to begin by considering a piece of evidence, very slight indeed from one point of view, yet extraordinarily significant if analyzed — I mean the character of the minds and temperaments most easily drawn towards Catholicism.

The present day is an exceedingly favorable period for the consideration of this point, since it is no longer fashionable, scarcely even traditional, to be a Catholic. Children of Catholic parents lapse from their religion with an ease hitherto unknown amongst her members; and conversions are usually made in the face of a kind of opposition that is seldom extended to those who would enter any other religious body. It is probably true that seldom if ever, except in the earliest times of the propagation of Christianity, or possibly at certain periods of persecution, has the standard of sincerity and thoughtfulness stood so high in the Catholic body as it stands to-day. Men do not drift to-day into Catholicism, and they drift out of it without much difficulty. There is no social influence at work in favor of Catholicism, and there is a good deal against it; and even amongst those who desire to be known as religious it is a good deal more fashionable, and considered a great deal more " spiritual," to stand outside creeds and churches than within them. It is always more pleasant to conceive of oneself as taught of God individually, as a mystically minded unit, than as a child who must go to school and form one of a crowd of other children. It is, then, an exceptionally favorable time to judge of the kinds of characters most deeply affected by the Church, whether attracted to or retained by her.

There is no question that, considered in general, two kinds of persons are drawn towards Catholicism and remain faithful to it.— the extremely simple and uneducated and the extremely shrewd and thoughtful. By "uneducated" I do not necessarily mean "unlettered"; by "shrewd" I do not necessarily mean "learned"; I mean rather the complete religious and philosophical amateur on one side, and the highly cultivated on the other. Neither do I mean that all the stupid people and all the clever are to be found amongst Catholics, and in no other company; but simply, that it is amongst these two classes, as a whole, that the characteristic Catholic is usually found. But the great mass of the tolerably thoughtful, the tolerably educated and intelligent, and more especially those who are content with their knowledge, and are unaware of its limitations — in fact, what may be called without offense the bourgeois mind remains completely unaffected. That this is so I think may be verified fairly satisfactorily by the condition of such countries as France or even

England, and by the testimony of priests who, after all, come directly into contact with statistics.

In France we have a remarkable state of affairs. On the one side there is a wide-spread defection from the Church; on the other hand, it is exactly these two classes of minds that have either remained in the fold or are returning to it. In the remote country districts both in north and south, in Brittany for example, and Lozère, fervor burns as brightly as ever, if not more ardently; many of the shrewdest intellects of the towns have remained entirely unaffected by " modern thought "; and the list of recent converts — including such names as those of Brunetière, Coppée, Paul Bourget, Huysmans, Retté — is surely a symptom of the same fact. " The deeper," says Pasteur, " I go into the mysteries of nature, the more simple becomes my faith. Already it is as the faith of the Breton peasant; and I have every reason to believe that if I am able to penetrate yet deeper, it will become as the faith of the Breton peasant's wife." Such testimony as this is surely a sufficient answer to those who say that " modern thought " has made it impossible for intelligent persons to be Catholics. It does not, of course, prove that the Catholic religion is true; but it shows that at any rate it is not as evidently false as the " bourgeois " intellect, which battens upon Haeckel and his school, desires to maintain. A man is perfectly at liberty to say that he does not believe the Catholic religion; but he cannot say, without very grave pride, in the face of such testimony as that of Pasteur, that it is obviously and evidently false, and that no intelligent person can believe it.

We have the same kind of evidence in England. Any English priest who has had any experience of converts would, I think, give the same answer. It is the absolutely simple and untechnical mind that produces one section of the converts; and the other section is drawn, for the most part, from markedly keen and able intellects. The mind most impervious to the Church's influence is that of the tolerably well educated — the young man who has studied a little, but not much, and that chiefly from small handbooks; the young woman who attends University Extension lectures, but not too many of them. For just as in social things the essential bourgeois is one who, being tolerably well off, is completely complacent with his position — unlike the lowest class which has no position to be complacent about, and the highest class which does not think about it at all either way; so in matters of mind. " How hardly shall they who *trust* in riches," says our Lord, " enter into the Kingdom of Heaven." Riches themselves are no obstacle; it is the bourgeois attitude towards them, whether

riches of wealth or intellect, that is really hopeless.
Complacency is the one obstacle to progress, in
finance, in art, in intellect, and in the things of the
spirit. To these may be added perhaps the
"academic mind," viz., that which is so deeply im-
mersed in one branch of knowledge that it is unaware that any other exists, that is so versed in
one science that it has come to think that phenomena irreducible to the formulæ of that branch, are
of no value as phenomena. For this too is another
kind of cosmic provincialism — that of the
"scribes and Pharisees" — against which our Lord
inveighs very bitterly.

Now, as we turn to the Gospels we find at the
very outset — (and I do not think one should dismiss this as fanciful, if one will but remember the
hypothesis on which we are speaking) — at the
very outset we find that it is from those two
classes that are drawn the first visitors to the cradle
of the Incarnate Word. It is the shepherds of
Bethlehem and the wise men from the East that
kneel there, the simplest and the wisest — the
simplest, those who are accustomed to silence and
stars and the elementary facts of birth and death,
those who have none of that knowledge that may
be so obscuring to clear vision; the wisest, those
who have reached the confines of wisdom as it
was then held — who, no doubt objectively con-

sidered, knew infinitely less of the physical world than the smallest school child of to-day, but who, subjectively considered, wére as highly trained and cultivated as the world could train and cultivate them, who were able to look back through the realms of knowledge they had penetrated and to understand how very little it all amounted to; these two classes, in fact, which, respectively, are not tempted to think that they know anything; and those who, by the acquiring of knowledge, have come to *know* that they do not know anything.

And I do not think that this illustration is fanciful; first, because on the Catholic hypothesis the Gospels, short as they are, contain what may be called a rough ground-plan of the Divine action on the world, and in a ground-plan negligible details find no room; and, secondly, because the ministry of Jesus Christ seems always to have been distinguished by the same characteristic. Those who followed Him seem to have been almost entirely drawn from these two classes. There were the fishermen on the one side — men, like shepherds, accustomed to manual work — that marvelous mind-cleanser — to silence, to stars and night and great spaces; and certain great doctors on the other — Joseph, Nicodemus, and the rest. And there stand out in that later band of apostles two great figures, as they stand in Rome to-day — Peter

and Paul. Peter, the scarred fisherman, talking
with a Galilean accent; and Paul, fresh from a
Greek-speaking university of a Roman town,
soaked in aristocratic traditions of religion, a
quoter of the Greek poets, accustomed to dialec-
tics.

Now this characteristic, true as it seems to be of
Catholicism, is markedly untrue of any other form
of religion with which I am acquainted. Certain
Indian religions, I believe, exhibit it to some extent; but it must be remembered that every Indian
religion that is at all Catholic in its scope has an
exoteric and an esoteric side — Buddhism notably so. It has, that is to say, one appeal to the
educated and another to the uneducated; and this
is not the case with Catholicism. Pasteur and the
Irish applewoman believe precisely and exactly
the same doctrines. All modern developments of
Protestantism, now that they have had their chance,
exhibit exactly the opposite to this characteristic of
Catholicism. Episcopalianism in Scotland, for instance, and, I am given to understand, in America,
is more or less an aristocratic religion, appealing
to lovers of beauty and refinement, but having little
influence upon the very poor. The same is certainly true of England, generally speaking, except
in the case of Ritualism (that form of Episcopalianism that has most in common with Rome),

and where associations or family ties or customs kept it in vogue. But even here it has very little dominating influence *as such* upon the lives of its adherents. It cannot be said to unite in a common fervor and devotion these two classes of minds of which I am speaking. As for the Nonconforming bodies, in England at any rate, their influence is almost entirely confined to certain ranks of society which are not, for the most part, either the most highly educated or the least.

Now the force of all this seems to lie in this direction. It seems to tend to show with tolerable power that all these other religions and forms of thought follow the exact lines which we should expect from human systems; each appeals, that is to say, to a particular kind of mind, and to be limited by natural boundaries. In the West, at least, each form of thought is attached almost irresistibly to a particular form of mind: the University man is, normally, an Anglican; the tradesman, normally, a Nonconformist; the member of the submerged tenth is occasionally a Salvationist, or he is nothing at all. There does not seem in non-Catholic Christianity to be any form of faith that appeals with equal force to all classes alike. Of course it is very difficult to prove this contention by accurate statistics, as it is difficult to prove anything at all by those means; but a rough estimate of its truth may be gained by quick bird's-eye views of average congregations. The ordinary Anglican congregation, when the purely conventional element has been removed, consists almost entirely of educated persons (except as has been noted in the case of Ritualism); the ordinary Nonconformist congregation, of the well-to-do tradesmen; and it is in Catholic churches alone that the scholar and the millionaire, and the well-born and the slum dwellers, sit side by side with mutual ease. There is one religion, and that the Catholic, that with every natural probability against it — since it is rigid in its uniformity and in its demands on faith, unflinching in its claims on bodily comfort, and transparently one under all circumstances — somehow succeeds in ignoring altogether the limits of any class or temperament, and appeals with equal force to the extremely cultivated and the extremely simple. When a Professor of Greek in one university, a Professor of Science in another — both middle-aged men — and a Judge on the Bench, famed for his keenness in sifting evidence, within the space of five years, after long thought, submit like little children to the Church, and kneel at the same altar-rail with their servants and the poorest Irish, you have reproduced a phenomenon practically unknown to other denominations — a phenomenon illustrated only by

that scene at Bethlehem to which I referred just
now. It appears to me, if I may say so in paren-
thesis, simply astounding that seeming Chris-
tianly minded people will actually bring it as a
reproach against the Church that it is, amongst other
things, the Church of the poor — of the Irish or
the Bretons. Certainly it is that, thank God;
though it also numbers among its adherents, as
we have seen, some of the keenest intellects of the
day. But to reproach the Church with being the
one Christian body that really holds the poor, is
to show an intellectual and spiritual snobbishness
before which one stands aghast and amazed. It is
to contradict in the most emphatic way some of
the most characteristic words of Jesus Christ,
" Blessed are the poor. . . . How hardly shall
the rich enter into the Kingdom of Heaven." If
there is one thing that marks the ministry of
Christ, and that indicates the Divine nature of His
teaching, it is His appeal to the poor. In fact,
it might be said that unless His teaching did indeed
appeal to the poor, it could not possibly claim to
be the religion of Humanity, since Humanity consists chiefly of the poor and uneducated. It could
not be the Sun shining from heaven on all alike,
if it did not illuminate the slums as well as the
parks. Light that is the prerogative of the rich
must always be artificial. And at the same time,

since it is certain that if there be Divine Truth anywhere in the world it cannot possibly conflict with human learning, it is a tremendous argument in favor of Catholicism that the Catholic creed is no less compatible with richness in knowledge than with poverty. An esoteric religion held only by the intellectual, an exoteric religion held only by the uneducated — neither of these can possibly be universally true; but a religion held by both, and in the same sense, at least must be independent so far of a merely mental and human origin. The argument does not demonstrate that the Catholic religion is true; though it creates at least a presumption that it is more than human; and it does demonstrate that no religion can be true which does not pass its test. Is not all this, then, exactly characteristic of what Divine Truth must exhibit if it visits the earth? It knows no boundaries of knowledge except those that men impose upon themselves; it draws irresistibly those who have no temptation to intellectual complacency, and those who by their very knowledge have overcome it; it fails to affect only those who, having learnt a little, think that they know all. So, to-day, it is largely the bourgeois minds who sit at home, who see nothing in the Heavenly Stable but the birth of one more of the children of men, who discuss the census, the House of Lords, the speeches of traveling politicians, the last smart sect, or the wild dreams of Haeckel, and think that these kinds of things are the pivots on which the world is turned.

II

THE HIDDEN LIFE

It must be remembered that, in discussing the characteristics of the Catholic Church, it is impossible to do more than to touch very lightly now and then upon the contrasts or resemblances to be found between her and the great non-Christian world-religions — Buddhism, Confucianism, Mohammedanism, and the rest. That there are these contrasts and resemblances is indisputable; yet it is impossible for one reason, if for no others, seriously to regard these rivals of hers as serious claimants to represent Divine Truth. It is an arguable proposition that there is no such thing as a Divine Revelation or a Divine Society — with that point I am concerned elsewhere, again and again, throughout these papers. My point here, however, is that if there be such a Revelation and such a Society, it cannot seriously be looked for in these world-religions. For they do not exhibit that characteristic which must mark the supreme Revelation whenever it appears — I mean the mark of serious and unfaltering proselytism. It is possible to understand how an exceedingly broad-minded human Society, which knows that it is only human, may deliberately refrain from missionary effort, believing that one kind of faith is good for one race, and another for another. But a Society that believes itself, rightly or wrongly, but sincerely, to possess the one Truth, cannot possibly rest content until it has done its utmost to convey that truth to all men. Now these Eastern religions have not even made the attempt to proselytize with any seriousness. If they do not claim, practically, by proselytism, this unique prerogative for themselves, how can it be claimed for them by others? Mohammedanism has done a little, with fire and sword, and so far has proved it own sincerity; but Mohammedanism has not attempted seriously to convert the West. Neither has Buddhism, ancient though it is. It has been in the world, its Western admirers delightedly tell us, for a quarter as long again as has Christianity; yet to-day, and always, from St. Thomas the Apostle downwards, it has been the Christian missionary who has bothered and disturbed the Buddhist — never the Buddhist the Christian. As for Confucianism, I do not suppose that there could be found five persons in any average thousand who could give even the vaguest sketch of its tenets. These religions simply do not possess what we may call Divine Self-consciousness; and therefore, although in many respects they have magnificent characteristics — notably this *Hiddenness* which I now propose to discuss — they surely are lacking in what the Divine Truth must have first and foremost, if it is Divine. Secondly, though this is comparatively a small point, we cannot keep noticing that the East, for all its religion, its patience, and its virtues, has not, as a matter of fact, developed as has the West. These developments are, many of them, deplorable no doubt; yet they are evidences of activity and life; and it is a remarkable fact, exactly in accordance with what we should expect, that Christianity, and Christianity only, has in the past proved the justice of Christ's simile of the leaven hidden in the dough. Human nature has seethed, bubbled and boiled, even to the overflowing of the pans, wherever Christianity has found entrance.[1]

The subject of the present chapter is the Hidden Life of the Catholic Church — the mark of Hiddenness, enjoyed certainly in a very deep degree

[1] This, however, is a very large subject, and I should like to refer all those who think that any of these religions have any kind of real claim to represent Divine Revelation to a very admirable book on the subject, written by the late Mr. Charles Devas, entitled *The Key to the World's Progress* (Longmans). For breadth of outlook, convincingness, and sweet reasonableness, as well as a real and technical knowledge of the subject, the book has no rival.

by certain Eastern religions, yet unaccompanied, in them, by that fierce and restless activity of proselytism, which must be its correlative and companion in any Society that claims to be Divine.

As we look round Western religions, whether forms of Christianity or not, we cannot help seeing that external activity — together, of course, with obviously necessary virtues — is considered almost the sole mark of a prosperous denomination. Certainly we Catholics heartily agree that it is one mark — that a religious Society that is inactive has no claim upon our attention; indeed, we Catholics are usually accused of too much zeal in this respect. But Catholicism stands alone, I think, in regarding its exact opposite — I mean retirement and contemplation — as being at least equally important; in fact, the Church goes even further than this, and tells her children that the life of complete seclusion, undertaken rightly, is the highest life that can be lived on earth. She permits, for example, any monk or nun professed to an active or semi-active life, to enter, without question, any contemplative order that will receive them; but not the reverse process. Here, too, it must be noticed, that such a life is not undertaken with a view to greater external activity afterwards; it is not retirement for the sake of rest and refreshment; it is the life in itself that is the object.

Now this is the extreme example of what may be called the element of "hiddenness"; but it is illustrated in innumerable other ways. The duty of every priest and every man in Holy Orders to recite the Divine Office every day in public or private — a duty occupying about one hour; the practice, though not the actual duty, of every priest to celebrate mass every day; the immense stress laid upon meditation and what is called "Recollection" in the case of the devout laity; the obligation of all alike to hear mass every Sunday — those and countless other similar points are all examples of what I mean. Some of these, no doubt, have a bearing upon the active life, but they are certainly not instituted to that end, nor, *primâ facie* at least, are they the most economical employment of time from this point of view. The object of them is the direct worship of God. When we add to this the enormous stress laid altogether upon the cultivation of the inner life — a cultivation brought to the very highest pitch in the branches of theology called Ascetic and Moral, we have a phenomenon singularly unlike that produced by any other form of religion. I do not mean, of course, for one instant that other denominations do not produce often exceedingly spiritual lives; but in the various systems, *as systems,* there is not anything like the same emphasis given to this point, nor any machinery so elaborate and so forcible as in the Catholic Church. Take the single point of the purely contemplative orders. Until comparatively recently in the Church of England there was not the smallest attempt to reproduce this life; and at the present moment I am acquainted with only two such attempts, comprising in their adherents not more than thirty souls all told. In other Christian bodies the very idea of such a life is despised and reprobated. So, too, with worship generally. In non-Catholic bodies there is not present the same obligation to worship God at stated times and in stated manners — in short, the direct worship of God, as distinguished from hearing sermons about Him, does not find the same place in other systems as in Catholicism.

Now the ordinary criticism of lives definitely consecrated to contemplation is perfectly familiar to us all. We are told that the hidden life is one of wasted powers; that " the man would be much more useful doing some honest work instead of shutting himself up and dreaming " — and all the rest of it. Now, as I propose to speak more at length on this point in a later chapter, I will not say much now, except to make two observations.

1. This hidden life is a marked characteristic of the Life of Jesus Christ in the Gospels. If we

believe that He was the Eternal Word of God, it appears to us at first sight simply inexplicable that that Word should have been silent for so long. He was to spend thirty-three years upon earth, and of those thirty-three He passed ten in silence, so far as the world was concerned, for every one of His public ministry. Further, even that public ministry itself was continually broken by silences. Again and again we hear of nights in prayer, and of withdrawals from the crowd. And, in the one incident in the Gospels where types of the Active and Contemplative lives, in the persons of Martha and Mary, are strongly contrasted, it is Mary, we are told, the silent worshiper, who has " chosen the better part," and who has " the one thing needful." If it is indeed a fact that Jesus Christ reproduces in His mystical Body that Life which He lived in the " days of his flesh," this huge and apparently disproportionate element of hidden-ness is exactly what we should expect from a Church in which He really lives. Even after the Incarnation itself there is still truth in the cry of the Old Dispensation, " Verily Thou art a God that hidest Thyself."

2. Secondly, this silence is again markedly characteristic of a Divine Fact dwelling on earth. If the Church were but a human Society, it would be inevitable that she should busy herself primarily

with humanity, that her highest commendation would be given (as indeed it is given in all other forms of Christianity) to those who are most active in ministering to the needs of men, that her workers should be judged by their activities and their external effectiveness, and that silence and retirement should only be commended so far as they ministered to such effectiveness. But if the Church is a Divine Society, if she looks always with inner but wide-open eyes upon celestial things, if she has the secret of eternity and dwells always seeing Him who is invisible, if indeed with angels and archangels she looks upon the Face of the Most Holy — this silence and absorption are simply inevitable and vital to her very existence. Certainly the eye cannot say to the hand —" I have no need of thee "; for the Divine Society has hands that must be work-worn as well as pierced; but neither can the hand have the nerve to labor without the guidance and inspiration of the eye. There must come moments when, as in heaven, there is " silence for about the space of half an hour " — there must be in this Body certain appointed cells and tissues, etherealized almost up to spirit, whose sole duty and vocation is this, to look upon the Face of God and rest absorbed there in that vision for which the human soul was designed. If men were but units, each designed to be *separately* perfect, there might be some justice in the charge that a Contemplative " wastes his life and powers "; but if the Church is an organic body, in which each cell vicariously lives for his neighbor (and, in fact, for the whole organism), it is perfectly reasonable that those cells should be differentiated and specialized. "If the whole body were the hand, where were the seeing?" And this specialized hiddenness, characteristic of the Sacred Humanity of Jesus Christ, is characteristic also only of one Christian Society; and is explicable only on the supposition that to her eyes this world is not all; that human needs are not always. the most imperative; that she lives, in fact, in the strength of a vision which none but she can fully perceive.

III

There are perhaps some half-dozen perpetually recurring problems by which the Church is continually faced — such questions as the use, and indeed the desirability of her wealth, her relations to politics and civil government, the right of her domination over individuals who do not formally belong to her. The problems in question arise nearly always out of the fact that she claims to be at once spiritual and temporal; supernatural and natural; a Heavenly Kingdom, yet living on the same platform as earthly kingdoms; Divine and human. On either side of her stand professedly spiritual bodies that have solved the tangle by cutting it. Quietists and non-Catholic mystics on the one side escape the problems by avoiding them, by standing aloof from the world altogether; Erastians have avoided the difficulties by becoming frankly human and civil. If the Church were spiritual only, or earthly only, her task would be comparatively easy; it is because she is both at once that she is continually in trouble.

Roughly speaking, her difficulties may be summed up under three heads.

1. The first is more or less speculative. How is it, it is demanded, that if the Church is really the Darling of God, He does not protect His own in a simple and earthly sense? Occasionally He seems to have done so, but far more often He appears to leave her to herself. The earthquake tumbles down the Catholic cathedral, the convent, the brothel, the Protestant temple, all in one common ruin. A revolution of infidels sweeps away a thousand Tabernacles at once; and the stipends of the priests who served them; and God's children are deprived of the Children's bread. And God makes no sign from heaven to protect her even in her most material needs. If the problem of pain and failure in general is insoluble, how far more insoluble is the perpetually recurring misery of her who professes to be His own!

Out of this speculative difficulty — a difficulty that surely has been responsible in the past for an enormous amount of distrust and even loss of faith amongst once ardent Catholics — arise a number of practical questions. To what extent may the Church avail herself of, or rely upon, earthly forces for her own preservation and prosperity? May or may not her missionaries appeal to gunboats for protection, and to large battalions in her wars?

If she were purely spiritual the answer would at once be — "No — My kingdom is not of this world." If she were purely earthly and human, her answer would be — "Yes — Let him that hath no sword sell his coat and buy one." But she is partly spiritual and partly earthly, or at any rate claims to be so; and there is no short answer at her disposal. Somehow or another she has to reconcile the paradox uttered indeed by her Founder at the beginning.

2. A second problem is also partly speculative, and concerns the question as to why God does not more frequently interpose with some miracle on behalf of her purely spiritual life. If it be really true that the Catholic Religion is God's Revelation, how easy would it be for Him to prove it so by unmistakable signs! If He truly desires the conversion of all men to the Catholic Church, why is it that He allows her miracles and signs to be reproduced by other bodies who do not possess the supreme truth? Why can Lourdes be, apparently, paralleled by psychological laboratories; and the morality of Catholics rivaled by the morality of Buddhists? Ought not the professed Founder of the Church to vindicate her superiority and uniqueness more convincingly?

And, again, from this arise practical problems. To what extent, if at all, ought the Catholic Church to rely upon miracles as means of converting the world? To what extent ought she to demand scientific investigation into her phenomena? To what extent ought she to demand from God visible and supernatural proofs of her mission; and to what extent would He support her if she did so? How is she to reconcile practically her Lord's two utterances —" These signs shall follow them that believe," and " Neither shall they be persuaded though one should rise from the dead "? If she were purely supernatural, or purely civil, the answer would be easy. If she were purely civil and human she would discount miracles altogether and rely merely upon those qualities and activities that cause other human societies to succeed; if she were purely supernatural, she might sit with her hands in her lap, and leave the rest to God; she could hardly trust in His miraculous interposition too much. But her difficulty arises from the fact that she claims to be both.

3. A third problem meets her in a thousand varying degrees, on almost every plane of her life; and it concerns the most fundamental relations of good and evil. It may be stated in a sentence. At what point does a lesser good become an evil? At what point does positive evil pass upwards into a lesser good? Let us state it in concrete form.

(a) It is acknowledged by all moralists that a

temporary " material evil " may occasionally be per-
mitted, if it is certain that any attempt to remove
it will result in a greater evil. If I see an obstinate
man, in good faith, doing something he ought not,
I am not always bound to inform him of it even
in the confessional, particularly if I know that my
information will not deter him from doing it. In
such a case my information will merely increase
his guilt.

(b) Yet there are so many exceptions to this
theory that the practical problem appears almost
insoluble. I cannot, for example, allow a callous
father to beat his child to death, however invinci-
bly ignorant the father may seem to be of his own
cruelty. And it is perfectly plain that I cannot,
a fortiori, allow a deliberate grave sin to continue,
even for the gaining of the greatest ultimate good.
I cannot let Judas go unrebuked to the high
priests, even though his going is a necessary step
in the process of the world's Redemption.

Now, the Catholic Church is continually faced
by concrete problems of this kind. " Look," cries
the world, " at the appalling amount of sin and
misery caused by the indissolubility of the marriage
tie. See that man with a wife incurably insane
in a lunatic asylum. Are not you Catholics simply putting a premium upon sin, simply compelling
that hot-blooded man to contract illicit unions in

bad faith, by this idealistic notion of marriage?
Why, again, should an innocent girl's life be
wrecked because in a moment of weakness she
consented to marry a lustful tyrant?"

Or again, it was urged very strongly at one time
upon Catholic missionaries in Japan to relax tem-
porarily the rigor of the sixth commandment.[1]
They were told — and with perfect reason — that
if they would but do this, their converts would
flock in by thousands. Is not the conversion of
Japan as a whole worth a few acts of sin done
in comparative ignorance?

Or again, how bitterly the Pope was blamed for
allowing wreck and ruin to fall upon the Church in
France, simply for the sake of a theory of Papal
jurisdiction! Surely, it was said, the theory
might be suspended for a few years until the crisis
was past; and then peace be made with honor and
prosperity to both sides.

And that sometimes even theologians can differ
with regard to this main problem is shown by the
divided opinions held at one time as to the point of
whether or no Chinese proselytes might be per-
mitted to practice ancestor-worship until they
learnt to realize by this means the full doctrine of
the Communion of Saints.

Now this kind of problem, like the other two,

[1] The Protestant "Seventh" Commandment.

arises from the Church's double nature. It is because she claims to be both divine and human that she has so often to arbitrate between the apparently conflicting Divine Rights of God, and the human rights and necessities of man. Somehow or another, because she stands on both sides, she has to reconcile both sides.

Now it would be impossible here to do more than indicate the problems and the reasons for the problems. To answer them would be to write a book on moral theology; for the solution of each depends upon innumerable circumstances and considerations peculiar to each. It is remarkable, however, to notice that these three main heads which I have described correspond precisely to those three crises described in the Temptation of Christ in the Wilderness, and arise from precisely parallel and even identical reasons. It is only on the hypothesis that Christ was both God and Man that He could be so tempted; it is only because the Church claims to be both Divine and human that she is tempted as was He. In a word, we have here one more illustration of the theme of these papers — viz.: that Jesus Christ is tempted in the Church to-day by the same arguments as in the wilderness, and for the same reasons.

1. *"If Thou be the Son of God, command that these stones be made bread."* " If you have come
6

into the world to redeem it, it is obvious that you must not die at the very outset of your mission. Use, then, your power to preserve your human life — that human life which is to be the medium of Redemption. If you do not use it you will die; and you will have shown that you are not the Son of God."

So the Tempter urges to the Church; and suggests to her that if she does not comply, or if God does not interfere, she is not what she claims to be.

" If you are really Divine, you ought not to allow your human side to be so overwhelmed by men's violence and earthly circumstance. Use all the powers at your disposal, because, however Divine you may be, you cannot be effective in the world except through your human effectiveness. Command that these stones be made bread. Use gunboats as spiritual weapons, whenever you possibly can."

Then follows the subtle suggestion, in the presence of catastrophe: —

" Surely you cannot be Divine, or God would not treat you so. If you were really Divine, the stones would become bread almost of themselves. At least they would cry out in your defense. But the heavens are as brass above you; there is no voice nor any that answers. . . ." And again follows the maddeningly skillful argument: " Be content, then, to be human, and to take your place with other human societies. Come down from the Cross, and we will believe."

And what is the answer? It is a reassertion of Divinity, and a simultaneous refusal to use it. " Man shall not live by bread alone." " It is true that I do live by bread — that I am human; but I am more than human, and am not therefore dependent upon it. It is true that I am an earthly Society, dependent upon earthly conditions for my effectiveness; but I am also Divine, and therefore not dependent upon them for my survival."

2. " *If Thou be the Son of God, cast Thyself down from a pinnacle of the Temple.*" " If you have come to convert men to a belief in your Divinity, convert them. Show a sign from heaven, an unmistakable and unique miracle, and they will believe."

" If you are truly a Divine Society, throw the responsibility upon God. Expect His interposition confidently. Make a simple act of faith, and surely He will respond with fire from heaven. . . . Ah! you are afraid that He will not. In fact, you know He does not. Then you are not really confident in your own Divinity after all. . . . Ah! take Him at His word. Surely His Angels will bear you up! Has He not said so?"

And the answer is an assertion of true Humanity.

" Thou shalt not tempt the Lord Thy God. . . .
I am here to work in human fashion, not to explode
celestial fireworks; to win men through their hearts
and their understandings and their wills, not to ob-
literate their manhood by an overwhelming exhibi-
tion of power. I gave free-will; I will not take it
away unless they give it freely. No sign shall be
given to this generation but the sign of the Prophet
Jonas — a Divine uprising from below, not a whirl-
ing descent from above. It is Lucifer who falls
like fire from heaven. It is God who is born as
a little child from below, to persuade, not to stun,
into submission."

3. *" All this will I give Thee if Thou wilt fall
down and worship."* " Here is your work visible
before you — to change these kingdoms of the world
into the Kingdom of the Lord and of His Christ.
And here, too, is a quiet place where, if any evil be
in what I ask, it will be but transitory and unknown.
Then perform this little material action of worship,
and accomplish at one stroke what must otherwise
occupy centuries, and involve an enormous and
wholly unnecessary expenditure of blood and tears."

So, too, to the Catholic Church.

" Here is the conversion of the world to be accomplished. Throw this grain of incense on Di-
ana's altar — a merely material action with no reality intended — and win toleration and a foothold

for yourself in the Roman Empire. Be silent about the most rigorous of all your rules for a few years, and gain Japan. Suppress one little principle concerning the constitution of your hierarchy, and keep your French Cathedrals and your wealth. No one will know. It will be a purely temporary arrangement. In a few years again, when all is quiet, you can reassert anything that you like. The crisis will be past."

And the answer: —

"Get thee behind me, Satan. . . . Thou shalt worship the Lord Thy God, and Him only shalt thou serve." "When once I do see plainly, in any given case, that actual right and wrong is involved, no consideration on earth shall make me swerve. Better the Rejection and the Cross a thousand times repeated; better the loss of every earthly aid and hope; better the loss of all things, than the destruction of one jot or tittle of the Law of God. It is the kingdoms of the world that are to be raised to the Kingdom of God; not the Kingdom of God degraded to the level of the kingdoms of this world. If I sacrifice the perfect Divine Plan in one detail, I do not save the world; and I lose myself."

Finally, notice that these three great temptations are temptations of strength, not of weakness. It is Christ's strength that is appealed to. "Assert Thy-

self. Save Thyself. Use Thy Power." It is the
Church's strength that is appealed to. " Use the
large powers at your disposal, natural and supernatural. And, you are so strong that you can af-
ford to be weak for one instant." And the answer
of both alike is the answer of St. Paul: " When
I am weak, then am I strong." " I faint often in
the wilderness, yet I do not die. All power is given
unto Me in heaven and earth; yet I choose to work
by human methods since I live amongst humanity.
I am willing to submit to the supreme shame and
failure of death and rejection; and I conquer through
the very elements which conquer Me."

And the answer is justified. On every earthly
hypothesis the Church ought to have died long ago
in the wilderness; yet she did not, since she lives
not by bread alone. By every argument the
Church's claim to supremacy in spiritual things ought
long ago to have been relinquished; yet new adherents pour in day by day. She ought long ago
to have perished through her refusal to make terms
with the world; she lost England three hundred
years ago, Rome forty years ago, and France yesterday, by her incorrigible obstinacy and foolish fidelity
to the Law of God. Yet, *Christus vivit; Christus
regnat; Christus imperat.* Angels have ministered
to her unknown and unperceived; though they have
not so far borne her up that she has not dashed her

foot against every stone.   Angels have served her, because of her very refusal to serve Lucifer.

Blessed, then, are the meek; for these shall inherit the earth.

IV

1. If there is one criticism which above all others springs to the lips of the non-Catholic observer, it is that the Catholic Church is too authoritative. We are told that human nature is a very variable and intricate thing; that one temperament can accept what another cannot; that what is true to one need not be true to another; that differences, whether of time or space, are sacred; that the fourteenth century cannot think as the twentieth; that the Neapolitan cannot believe as the German; in fact, that Truth, although one, has innumerable aspects and facets, and that any attempt to evade this fact, and to impose one set of dogmas on all men alike, must end either in failure or intellectual tyranny. The Catholic Church therefore is declared to be the enemy of Truth, for this is precisely what she attempts to do. She dares to proclaim one creed for all alike; to fetter free inquiry; to make no allowance for points of view; to be the bitter enemy of all progressive science, which, she fears, may overturn her own credibility; to silence and condemn

those of her accredited ministers who show any independence of thought.

Certain other bodies then are held out to us as our examples. The Anglican Communion, for instance, is, by many of her adherents, proclaimed to be the most adequate exponent of real truth, since she makes allowances for these various points of view, and is content to drive her team with a comparatively loose rein. She permits, for example, some of her ministers to teach a creed practically indistinguishable from the Catholic, others a creed equally indistinguishable from a kind of moderate Calvinism, and a third party to hold elements of both with the extreme characteristics of neither. She herself then allows — and is frequently commended for allowing — this broad divergence on points of faith and practice, and refuses to decide them. It is of no use for the Ritualist to say on one side, or the Low Churchman on the other, that each, respectively, truly represents her and that the other is disloyal. Neither is it possible for even the Moderate Churchman to claim that he, as representing the golden mean, represents her to whom the "golden mean" is, notoriously, an ideal. For so long as she permits these various schools to represent her she permits all their views, and, simultaneously, implicitly denies that any one set of them is *de fide*. Her "Voice," then, is perfectly intelligible, in spite of what some controversialists have said; and its message is that there is no certainty on these matters. She may, justly, take on her lips Mr. Bernard Shaw's epigram, and repeat, "The Golden Rule is that there is no Golden Rule." Others tell us that even the Anglican Church is too strict — that the Articles of Religion, for example, impose an unjustifiable burden upon the clergy, and the Athanasian Creed upon the laity; they bid us look to more loosely knitted societies as the real patrons of truth. Others, again, tell us that all societies are too strict; that every man must have his own religion if he is to be loyal to his own conscience; that no dogmas can be final and no creed irreformable. We must continually be bringing our theology up-to-date, if it is to command the belief of thinking men. All, however, whatever their other differences, are united in this — that the Catholic Church, from her rigidity, her formulæ and her unchangingness, must obviously and evidently be wrong.

Now, all these criticisms are perfectly admirable from the non-Catholic standpoint. If Truth is a relative thing — if the nearest approach we can make to Truth is to sift the opinions of those most competent to speak upon religion — if, in a word, Truth is something merely arrived at by man's efforts, all those criticisms are just. In that case we do need, first, National Churches for those who are willing to class themselves loosely with their fellow-countrymen; we need Congregational bodies for those groups who desire something more exactly suited to their particular temperament; and we need Individualism in religion for those who go even further and wish to verify individually each single doctrine to which they give their assent.

As human societies only, these groups of believers are acting very prudently and justly in forming associations for the study of truth, for the worship of God, and for the propagation of their opinions; and they are prudent as well as charitable in allowing great latitude to independent thinkers who cannot exactly range themselves under any set of formularies. But if Truth is something different from all this — if it is a body of facts revealed by God, then the entire position falls to the ground. If Truth is an objective reality, the same for all, parties and schools of thought become meaningless. We do not have schools of thought on the subject of the orbit of the earth, or the existence of the animal creation; and we put persons who doubt the existence of these things into the nearest lunatic asylum.

Now, when we turn to the Life of Christ in the Gospels, we find that authoritativeness and finality were the characteristics of His teaching which most impressed those who heard Him. The people of His day were accustomed to " schools of thought " and " aspects of truth," exactly as we are in our own. Each great doctor and Rabbi had his own set of pupils; the commonwealth of Jerusalem had, in spite of the original Revelation which, it was claimed, Moses had received at the beginning, passed into very much the same state as that in which our own commonwealth finds itself. There was developing amongst them (as indeed amongst all human religious societies, sooner or later), from the single premiss that men are individual, the conclusion that men's perceptions of Truth (and therefore ultimately Truth itself) are individual, too; or, in other words, that since men's perceptions of Truth are subjective, Truth is practically subjective also. There were the precisians for the Law, the Pharisees, the aristocratic separatists, men of the highest probity of life, who observed unfalteringly the whole Law of God, as they understood it, down to its minutest details. There were the Sadducees, also of the " high " mode of thought, with distinctive views upon eschatology; the Herodians — the national or Erastian party — the Zealots, the Essenes, and the rest. Each party had a right to exist, each was recognized in its own degree; and upon this exceedingly human state of affairs descended One who dared to say in the very Temple of God where the schools competed: "If any man thirst, let him come unto Me and drink"— who stretched His hands to those burdened with disputings, with the distractions of labor, with the consciousness of failure, in short, with that whole intolerable weight which human nature, left to itself, sooner or later finds upon its shoulders; and to say: "Come unto Me all you that are weary and heavy-laden, and you shall find rest to your souls. For My yoke is sweet and My burden light." "I am the Way, the Truth and the Life. No man cometh unto My Father but by Me." "This or that was said unto you by them of old time; but I say unto you — something else." This, then, was the comment passed upon Him by those who, after all, are the best qualified to judge — the "common people "— those heralded by the shepherds and captained by the fisher-apostles from the North. "The common people," we read, "heard Him gladly; for He taught them as one having authority, and not as their scribes and Pharisees."

Now, confidence in claiming to be, or even to possess, the Truth, is not an absolute proof of the justice of the claim. Most founders of new schools of thought claim it usually sooner or later, though, as St. Augustine says in the passage previously quoted, none has ever claimed it so vehemently as did Jesus Christ. But, certainly, the other proposition is true, that if there is such a thing as a Divine Teacher anywhere, He must have this confidence in its most extreme form. Human societies, or merely human authorities of any kind, will always show from time to time a certain faltering in the face of the world's demand: sooner or later the note of hesitation will make its appearance. The Divine Teacher alone will make the claim consistently and always. The Divine Teacher alone will retain always the confidence with which He begins; for the Divine Teacher alone has the Divine Self-consciousness necessary for such a claim. It will be characteristic of the Divine Teacher always to teach as One having authority and not as Scribes and Pharisees. He will seem to the cautious world intolerably positive and imperious.

Now, when we cast a bird's-eye view back in perspective, as well as round us at the present day, we find but one such continuous claim made with the utmost confidence always, from the day when Jesus Christ first stepped out on the world's stage with that challenge to the world; and we find but one Society which has ever succeeded in eliciting such absolute and blind faith as must be expected from those who recognize a Divine Teacher; to one Society and one Society only is that pathetic cry of St. Peter in his bewilderment continually uttered, " To whom shall we go? Thou hast the

words of Eternal Life." And it is this same Society that alone is distinguished by the reproach of
all other seekers after truth, that she teaches as if
she herself had the sole prerogative of teaching,
that she dares to say in face of the infinite varieties
of human experience — "I have — or rather I am
— the Truth, the whole Truth, and nothing but the
Truth. Come unto Me, then, and find rest." It
is this one Society which in face of the universal
idol of broad-mindedness, and tentative hesitation,
and "Modern Thought," and endless toleration,
dares still to condemn as well as to justify; to cast
those whom she considers faithless out of her pale,
as well as to gather in the weary and self-burdened;
to be fiercely exclusive, as well as singularly in-
clusive.

It is worth while, then, to consider whether this
amazingly Divine Self-consciousness, this unique
and unfaltering claim, this air of proclamation rather
than the air of laborious research, is not precisely
what we should expect from a Teacher truly come
from God — whether there is not evident in all this
an unmistakable aroma of Divinity such as Peter
himself detected when he cried, "*Tu es Christus!*
Thou art the Christ, the Son of the Living God."

2. We have not time in these few pages to discuss
at any length the identity of the dogmatic teaching
of Jesus Christ and of the teaching of the Catholic

Church. That alone, together with the necessary discussions on what is known as " development of doctrine "— that aspect of the living truth to which Christ refers when He speaks of the Kingdom of Heaven resembling the elaborate growth and development of a tree from the seed — all this, by itself, would occupy the whole of our space; but before passing on I would like to draw attention to four short points in this teaching by which we can gauge the astonishing identity of that doctrine then and now, as well as the equally astonishing identity of the world's attitude towards that teaching.

We have just seen the manner of His teaching to be unique and startling; but the substance of His doctrine was no less startling.

There are four occasions in our Lord's life when the objections of His critics take a sudden and almost dramatic form.

The first is the criticism of Nicodemus towards certain words of our Lord upon the Baptism by water; and it shapes itself in the exceedingly human phrase —" How can —? How can a man be born when he is old? "

The second, in order of thought, was the criticism of the doctors towards His words concerning the forgiveness of sins; and again we recognize the human ring of the voice —" Who can forgive sins save God only? "

The third concerns His words upon a " Living Bread " that He will give from heaven; and again the phrase recurs —" How can this man give us His flesh to eat? "

Finally, all three are summed up in a criticism that takes the form of stones, since verbal objections are useless in the face of such an horror —" Before Abraham was, I AM. . . . Then took they up stones to cast at Him."

Now, if the average critic of Catholicism selected in haste the first four most obvious objections in his mind against the substantial truth of the Catholic religion — the first (as he would call them) " commonsense " objections — I think that in ninety-nine cases out of an hundred they would correspond almost precisely with these objections recorded in the Gospels.

First, he would say, the sacramental system generally is all wrong. No intelligent man, he would say, at the present day can possibly be expected to believe that any merely external rites can possibly affect that mysterious inner thing which we call spiritual life. Character, he would say, has its own laws of growth and development, its inevitable movements and energies and activities. Sacraments and the rest may be beautiful symbols and object lessons — pictures, though comparatively coarse and inaccurate — of the action of God upon the soul; but

7

they cannot possibly be more. We go forward, he would say, from childhood to maturity, profiting by our good actions, losing by our evil actions, under the reign of a steady and verifiable law from beginning to end. There can be no sudden movement from without that can affect us essentially, no interruption to the orderly action of the universe. "How can a man be born again, when he is old? Can he enter a second time into his mother's womb, and be born? How can a man begin all over again from the beginning, just because he has submitted to an external ceremony?"

If you press the critic a little further you would find that he particularly objected to the doctrine of absolution. Surely, he would say, the affairs of a man's soul are his own and God's, and no one else's. If we sin against God (and the malice of all sin, so called, is that it is against God), surely that is God's affair and the sinner's; the system of the confessional is absurd and contradictory of all solid truth, as well as morbid and enervating. In a word —" Who can forgive sins save God alone?"

Press him a little further; and, as he warms to his work, he will presently lay his finger upon that which is the very heart of the Catholic system — the belief of Catholics that Jesus Christ truly and indeed gives His disciples His flesh to eat. He could stand anything else, he says, perhaps, but not this. He has a great admiration for the Catholic Church in many ways; he admires her philanthropy, her zeal — even her worship; but this doctrine is a final and insuperable obstacle. He can understand it as a symbol, he realizes its emotional appeal; but as sober fact it is too much. " Many therefore of His disciples hearing it, said: This saying is hard, and who can hear it? . . . How can this man give us His flesh to eat? . . . After this many of His disciples went back, and walked no more with Him."

Finally, our critic would probably sum up all his objections under the heading we have already discussed at full. It is the Divine Self-consciousness of the Church that he finds the final obstacle. He would tolerate her if she consented to be one among many, if she would take her place with the other religious bodies of the world and meet them as equals; but her supreme arrogance is her condemnation. For this arrogance, if considered carefully, is nothing less than a claim to be actually Divine. To teach with such confidence as this means, simply, that she who so teaches believes herself indwelt by Divinity: Infallibility asserts that; Excommunication implies it. It is to claim that she exists in the very mind of God; that she has access to His secret counsels; that she is older than the world; that she was before Abraham; that she is in a sense the very Eternal Himself; that what she binds on earth is bound in heaven; that what she looses on earth is loosed in heaven. . . . " Then took they up stones to cast at Him."

Now, it is not my object in these papers to discourse on Catholic doctrine in detail, nor to answer the numerous and often very sensible objections that non-Catholics bring against what they conceive to be the belief of Catholics; and in any case there would not be time to discuss these particular doctrines in question. I have only quoted these passages in support of my thesis that Jesus Christ is the same yesterday and forever; and that so is the world. What He taught then, His Church teaches now; what men said then, men say now, often in the same words. I remember a Protestant procession in England intended to demonstrate against the claims of Catholic doctrine to be Scriptural; and upon the banner of the procession was inscribed, with pathetic simplicity, the very sentence uttered by the Pharisees against one of these doctrines — " Who is this that speaketh blasphemy? Who can forgive sins save God alone?" So a murderer might shelter himself under the example of another Scriptural character, and write over his bed in the condemned cell —" Am I my brother's keeper?"

So an atheist might quote Scripture to the effect that "there is no God." [1]

Lastly, on this point I would like to draw attention to one more single consideration. It is a fact that our Lord said these things; it is a fact that the Catholic Church says them now. It is further a fact that the things in question are, to all appearances, clean against the human experience of the rest of the world. I would ask you to consider whether the very magnitude of these claims, and the astonishing unanimity of 250 millions of Catholics in believing them — whether the consciousness that could utter such words, and the power that somehow or another has succeeded in making this uncountable multitude of souls of all centuries, temperaments, attainments, and nations, believe them, not only as academic formulæ or philosophical statements, but as the very arteries and sinews of their spiritual life — that has made so many not only die for the doctrines, but (what is much harder) live for them and by them — is there not in all this the very strongest presumption for thinking that such a consciousness and such a Power cannot be less than divine? It seems impossible to make men of one nation agree even on political doctrines; but it has been found possible by the Catholic Church to make men of all nations agree on religious doctrines. When I was a student in the

[1] Ps. liii. 1.

University of Cambridge, I used often to find in one lecture-room men of one nation and six religions. When I became a student in the University of Rome, I found in one room men of six nations and one religion. . . . Is it conceivable that it is a merely human power that makes such a thing possible?

V

MIRACLES

We pass on to a further characteristic of Catholic life — the element of the miraculous. And first and foremost it is necessary to point out, that, with the exception of one or two recent sects which do not even attempt to claim historical continuity with the Life of our Lord, there is not one form of Christianity at the present day that even desires to compete with Catholic Christendom in this matter. It is in fact the reproach against the Church in the mouths of most persons who delight in calling themselves " plain men " and " commonsense thinkers " that she has committed herself irreparably to a belief in the constitution of the world and to possible interferences with that constitution, which renders her altogether discredited in the light of the twentieth century. Let us sum up their criticisms on the matter.

1. Until recently it was said simply that the incidents did not happen. Men simply were *not* restored to health by the prayer of a saint; eyes were not opened; paralysis was not cured; diseases were

not vanquished, at so-called holy wells and shrines; levitation was not a fact; communications were not made at great distances except by physical means. And it was obvious, therefore, that those persons who said they did happen were either unscrupulous and dishonest knaves, or fools so blinded by superstition and nervous excitement as to be wholly unworthy of credence.

2. Within the last thirty or forty years, however, a complete *volte-face* has been performed. No average scientist forty years ago believed that those things happened; no average scientist to-day dreams of doubting them. What is wrong with the Church now, though, is her explanation of the incidents. Of course the things happen, or at any rate most of them; they happen in every hypnotic hospital; they are accomplished by people without the least shadow of faith in Divine power. The whole affair, in fact, is a matter of psychology; there is nothing whatever supernatural about it. So-called miracles, therefore, are of no value whatever in establishing the truth of Religion. It is true that the Church did happen to be in the right, after all, as regards the negligible detail of Facts; she did, as a matter of fact, succeed in observing and recording quite tolerably and accurately that which altogether escaped the notice of scientists; she did, after all, manage somehow or other to secure and use the secrets of

psychology and suggestion several centuries before
the words existed or the sciences were dreamed of;
but that does not at all derogate from her dishon-
esty now in attempting to exploit what are known
to be perfectly natural phenomena for her own ends.

The contemplation of these facts is highly in-
structive and interesting. We were wrong fifty
years ago in our relations of events; and now that
we are proved to be right in that matter, we are
wrong in our explanation of them. In any case we
are wrong, if not dishonest. It is interesting to
reflect that even more recently the Catholic belief
that two personalities could, in extreme cases, in-
habit one body, has been very considerably recognized by scientists; only it is called "Alternating
Personality" in order to do away with the possibility
of believing anything so grossly superstitious as the
existence of discarnate personalities, commonly
called Demons.

Before looking into the matter further, let us
turn to the records of the Gospel. Two or three
important considerations emerge.

1. Jesus Christ claimed that the truth of His
Divine Mission was corroborated and sustained by
supernatural happenings, by His control over nature. "Believe Me," he says, "for the very works'
sake."

2. He promised to His disciples that the same

sanctions should accompany their Mission as had accompanied His. " Greater works than these shall ye do, because I go to the Father."

3. These apparently supernatural events were commented upon and rejected in terms and for reasons almost precisely parallel to those with which Catholic miracles are met.

Either they did not happen, or they were done through some power other than that which their Worker declared to be behind them. The man born blind who professed to have been cured by Jesus Christ could not possibly have been born blind; otherwise he could not have been cured. And, finally, he must be a very wicked person, and therefore untrustworthy. Or, when every other explanation failed, those possessed by devils and released by this same upstart Prophet, were declared to be released by the sinister powers of darkness, and not by the Power of God. It is true that this explanation of Catholic miracles has not up to the present been advanced by scientific critics, but surely this is only because their recent advance in study has not yet brought them to the point of believing in the Devil: the explanation has been frequently urged by less well-educated critics of a more simple faith.

4. Since these miracles, then, were alleged to be unsatisfactory as evidence of Christ's Divine Mission, it was asked of Him that He should perform

some unmistakable sign from heaven, something that could not be gainsaid; and to this He answered with very clear indignation that no sign should be given except the sign of the Prophet Jonas — in a word, the Resurrection; and even this, He said, would prove insufficient. " Neither will they be persuaded if one should rise from the dead." This prediction was exactly fulfilled when the empty tomb confronted the incredulous. " The disciples came by night," they said, " and stole Him away."

Let us sum up these considerations in a more compact form.

A certain set of phenomena — unusual, at any rate — has accompanied both the inauguration of Christianity and its continuous life ever since in Catholicism. Practically no other forms of Christianity have been distinguished by this mark; in fact, the very claim is not made. *Primâ facie,* therefore, Catholicism in this matter, as in the others of which we have spoken, has an exceptional right to be considered as a true continuation of the religion of the Gospels, since the Founder of Christianity expressly predicted that His true disciples should be so distinguished. So far, therefore, as regards the dispute between Catholicism and Protestantism, it is somewhat pathetic to hear those non-Catholic Christians, who acknowledge freely the miraculous element in the Gospels, striving to explain the absence of that element in Protestantism, in spite of the fact of Christ's own words on the matter. We are told, for example, that miracles were necessary for the establishment of Christianity, but not for its continuation, in spite of the fact that in every heathen country of the world exactly the same need for miracles is found now as was found at the beginning. And, as regards the Catholic claim that miracles are continued amongst the true followers of Jesus Christ, Protestants are forced, in the discounting of this claim, to side with the opponents of all miracles, and to use the same kinds of arguments against them as the avowed enemies of our Lord used against His own.

With regard, however, to the dispute between Catholicism and the rest of the world — between those, that is, who accept both Christ's miracles and those of the Church and those who deny both or explain them away by natural means, the controversy is far more serious. It is alleged by this latter class, either that the incidents did not happen — though this is a position that is being very swiftly abandoned by all educated persons who have the very slightest acquaintance with medicine or psychology; — or else that they did happen — at least many of them; but that they are of no value as evidential marks of religion, since they can be reproduced by natural means, and are performed under the patronage of other religions besides the Catholic.

Now before passing on to the intentions of Christ in performing these, at least, abnormal feats, it is necessary to make one or two remarks on this latter explanation of the miraculous in general.

1. As has been pointed out, after all it was the Church which was right, and " scientific " opinion wrong as to the objective facts. Those who were dismissed, until recently, either as dishonest or as hysterical visionaries, have been proved to have been more accurate in their observation, and wider in their experience, than their scientific critics. This is a suggestive thought.

2. Again, as has been pointed out, it is remarkable that, if the naturalistic explanation is true — (and of course no Catholic would dream of denying that there is a *modicum* of truth in it)— somehow or another for two thousand years Catholic sanctity has been using and applying forces simply unknown and undreamed of by the scientific world. Even at the present day there are certain non-Christian doctors who acknowledge that what is called " Religious Suggestion " is probably the most powerful of all forms of Suggestion. What then is this strange element distinguishing Religious Suggestion from other forms

of suggestion? And what has been the secret by which Catholics have somehow stumbled upon forces of which the rest of the world has, for the most part, known little or nothing?

That there is some truth in the explanation by Suggestion has been always acknowledged, of course, under other terms, by Catholics, and indeed is indicated by Christ Himself. Again and again in His own miracles He has insisted that it is Faith which has made them possible. Even His own power was restrained by a strong environment of incredulousness. "He could do no mighty work there," we read, "because of their unbelief." But this element of Faith does not exclude the other element of the Power on which Faith fastened. In one "mighty work"— the healing of the woman who touched His garment — the two are expressly spoken of: "Virtue is gone out of Me," He cried at one moment, and, at the next, "Thy faith hath saved thee." The two therefore are in the relations (as has been said) of a bow to a violin. Neither, in itself, is ordinarily productive of music; each requires its complement. And if it is one-sided, on the one hand, to attribute all to the violin — all to the sovereign power of God, it is as equally one-sided, on the other — as is the habit of modern psychological amateurs — to attribute all to the bow — all to the apprehensive grasp of Suggestion.

3. A third point is, that all the psychological explanations in the world cannot possibly cover all the alleged incidents, unless a very simple and childlike act of faith is made by the psychologists in question. For instance: There are certain incidents at Lourdes and elsewhere, undoubtedly acknowledged to have taken place (for example, the instantaneous cure of the leg of Pierre de Rudder, broken for eight years)— which simply cannot be reproduced by all the psychological explanations in the world. Again and again remarkable cures take place — for instance, the recent cure of Marie Borel — which might conceivably be brought about by strong Suggestion, but never within the amazingly short space of time in which the cures are actually accomplished. (I am speaking now of cures which simply are not disputed at all by anyone whatever.) How then do psychologists meet these phenomena? They meet them, as I have heard with my own ears, by what Catholics would call an "act of faith," so sublime and so simple that no Breton peasant could surpass it for childlike trust. "I believe," say these scientific psychologists, "in Nature. All that is done is done by Nature. But Nature has her secrets; and these

are some of them. When I know more I shall understand how it is done. At present I can only believe and trust." Truly this is magnificent; but it is not Science. It is Faith.

4. Fourthly, there is one general remark on the miraculous as a whole that should be made before considering Christian miracles in particular.

It is advanced against the whole claim that Science has revealed to us the reign of Law; that more and more we are tending to find that all phenomena are produced by law; and that therefore these supposed infringements and interruptions of Law are becoming unthinkable to all scientific minds.

But who in the world ever claimed that miracles involve the breaking or infringement of Laws? It is one of the clauses of the Law of Gravitation that all solid bodies tend to fall towards the center of the earth. But I do not infringe the Law of Gravitation by lifting a book from a table — I bring another law into force which supersedes, for the time being, or overrides the Law of Gravitation. Now Catholics do not claim that the Lawgiver is forced to break or infringe His own laws when He performs a miracle, but simply that He brings some supernatural force or Law to bear, that for the time being overrides natural law. Catholics claim, in other words, that the Creator is greater than the Creature — that He has certain realms of energy at His disposal of which we know little or nothing, and that He draws upon this energy to do certain actions in a manner which we cannot, according to our present knowledge, explain. There is nothing whatever unscientific about this, whatever may be its truth or its falsehood. But the non-Christian quasi-scientific method of arguing is just one more instance of the almost incredible provincialism and parochialism of our own days. Scientific persons are not compelled to believe in Christianity unless they consent to do so; but at least they might have learnt (and really scientific persons do learn) the elements of natural humility. The attitude of these quasi-scientists seems to me to resemble the old woman in England who believed without a tremor when her son told her that he had found timbers from the ark upon the top of Mount Ararat; but who indignantly refused to believe him when he said he had seen fish flying in the air. " Fish do not fly in the air," she said, " they swim in the water. Therefore you cannot possibly have seen flying fish."

Let us now turn, however, to miracles as a whole, whether those recorded in the Gospels or in history, and see whether there is not some principle in their intentions which may tend to clear up this agelong confusion as to their evidential value. Let us begin again with a parable.

8

I have a great personal friend, let us say, whom I know intimately in all kinds of ways. Among other things I have the run of his papers and am acquainted with his banking account; and I happen to know that he is of an extremely generous disposition and does good by stealth.

One day I am told in the street that he has given a donation of £1000 to a charitable fund: I am told this on tolerable, but not absolutely unimpeachable authority; but it is so entirely in accordance with what I know of my friend's general character, that I have not the smallest difficulty in believing it. A third person, however, who knows my friend only slightly, upon hearing the same rumor from the same source, at once expresses his disbelief in it. It is not in the least like him, he says; his name never appears in lists of charitable donations. The story is obviously untrue. A few days later, however, he is certified that it is a fact; and he then declares that the money must have been given for an unworthy motive. There must be some explanation behind; perhaps it is blackmail; perhaps it is for the sake of advertisement; perhaps the man is mad.

Now this seems to me a very tolerable parallel to the case of miracles.

It is said that they only convince those who are convinced on other grounds of the truth of Religion. I think that that is, generally speaking, quite true. There is not one instance of an avowed enemy of our Lord being convinced of His Divinity by any miracle; and there is probably not one well authenticated instance of a similar event in the case of any Catholic miracle. For it seems to be undoubtedly a fact that God never has yet consented to perform such an overwhelmingly obvious marvel that free-will no longer has free play. Our Lord refused to do so at least twice in His earthly life. He never absolutely coerces free-will; He never crushes (in a word) the supreme endowment of man. Miracles seem to be of such a nature that it is just possible for one morally indisposed to believe — one who is completely out of sympathy with God — to frame an explanation that will dispose of their evidential value. Miracles, both in the Gospels and in the Church, are of such a character that they elicit culminating acts of faith in the hesitating, and confirm and strengthen faith that is beginning to falter. Further, they supply additional evidence to the claim that their worker is Lord over nature; but they do not utterly coerce and crush out of existence the free-will of a man whose whole moral disposition is against faith — one who, on other grounds, is out of sympathy with God. Each side has a certain right to claim to be logical; just as I myself and the third party of my parable have a right to claim logic in our interpretation of the story about our friend. I, knowing my friend, find that the reported donation is completely in line with what I know of him on other grounds, even though it is abnormal that he should publish his name in this instance; the story gives me just one more emphatic proof that he is a generous and open-hearted man. It is not merely sentiment; it is a real and logical proof. The third person, however, has, on other grounds again, formed quite another opinion of my friend; and he begins, therefore, by disbelieving the story. When, however, the story is shown to be true, he very reasonably sets about finding some explanation that will cover it.

So then with miracles. Catholics, on a thousand moral grounds, believe in the Catholic Church. They are convinced that she is what she claims to be. The disciples of Christ, on originally quite other grounds than His miracles, came to the conclusion that He was more than Man. When, therefore, Catholics hear of miracles — when the disciples saw the blind healed and the lepers cleansed — both alike, quite reasonably and logically take the miracles to be confirmatory proofs of what they already know. And those who look on, not yet disciples, but in moral sympathy with the Wonder-

Worker, are encouraged and helped towards Faith by the same incidents.

Those, on the other hand, who were convinced that our Lord was an impostor — those who are convinced to-day that the Catholic Church is a sham and a fraud — those begin by denying the facts. This man could not have been born blind; the other could not have been possessed by a devil; or if he was possessed, he is still possessed. When, however, the fact of the cure is established, they look about for explanations other than the Christian. It was done by the power of Beelzebub; it was done by mere religious suggestion. It proves nothing at all.

For, after all, it is very difficult to frame any miracle that *cannot* be explained away. If a certain type of modern psychologist saw a man raised from the dead, he would say either that the man was not dead, or that he was not raised. Either it was a fraud, or an illusion. If he saw the Heavens opened and Christ sitting on the Right Hand of the Majesty on high, the papers would be full of headlines next morning, describing the remarkable configuration of clouds, caused, no doubt, by the tail of a comet. We see the same type of determination not to believe among certain schools of Biblical criticism. When the four

Evangelists appear to differ minutely in their narrations of the same event, it is a proof that they are untrustworthy and inaccurate; when they precisely agree, it is proof that they have copied from one another, and therefore are untrustworthy again! Heads I win; tails you lose!

Nothing therefore will convince the unconvincible. "They have Moses and the Prophets," says our Lord. "They have the Law they are always talking about, pointing them straight to a Lawgiver; they have Prophets — men whose eyes are opened, whose words are flame and fire, whose glance is inspiration; they have the moral witness; they have the vision waiting for the pure in heart; they have Moses and the Prophets, the Rule and the Exception — Nature and Supernature — kindling in every sunset, vibrating in the instincts of every heart — If they believe not Moses and the Prophets — neither will they be persuaded, though one rose from the dead."

Summary of Previous Chapters.

Before passing on to the next section it will be as well to sum up very shortly the points of identity, already discussed, between Christ and His Church.

1. We began by considering the type of mind from which most sincere Catholics to-day are

drawn. They are the Shepherds and the Kings; they are as Peter and Paul. They are the very simple, and the very deep. And this is exactly what we should expect to find among the followers of Divine Truth. Other forms of religion are drawn almost entirely from one class or another. There is no denomination, except the Catholic, that really unites such men as Pasteur, and Huysmans, and Lord Brampton, and Father Cortie, and Professor Windle, on one side, and Biddy Maloney, and Jack Smith, and the negro, and the Neapolitan on the other. For notice that it is actually one Religion that unites them; they believe actually the same things. There are no exoteric and esoteric departments in the Catholic Church. It is natural for human societies to appeal to one class or another; it is natural for a Divine Society to appeal to all classes, except to the *bourgeois* mind which thinks it has reached the confines of knowledge just because it has not; and to the specialist mind which thinks that its own science is exhaustive of truth. Therefore to-day as in Bethlehem, the bourgeois sits at home and discusses the Census, while Shepherds and Kings adore in the Stable. As it was in the beginning is now and ever shall be.

2. Next we discussed the mark of Hiddenness. As thirty out of thirty-three years of our Lord's Life were passed in seclusion; so it is character-

istic of the Catholic Church alone to regard the
life of seclusion and devotion to be even more
august than the life of activity. Human societies
naturally regard human activities as the supreme
duty; but the Divine Society that endures seeing
Him who is invisible, regards all merely human
activity as comparatively provincial and parochial
when contrasted with those enormous and Eternal
Interests, that immense silence of Heaven in which
sooner or later all noises must sink to rest. It is,
then, one of the unique characteristics of Divine
Truth on earth, that Heavenly things should, to
her eyes, loom larger than earthly.

3. Next we noticed the various problems continually besetting the Church's life on earth; and
saw how they arose from her double nature of
heaven and earth. If she were either wholly supernatural or wholly natural, they would be no temptations at all, for they are all aimed, so to speak,
at her waterline; each of them is an attempt to
confuse her between the claims of God on one side
and of man on the other; each of them gains its
acuteness from her position on both sides. How
far may she use earthly means for heavenly ends?
How far may she rely upon Divine interposition?
How far may she go in tolerating a lesser good
for the sake of an ultimate greater good? And
we saw, moreover, that these three kinds of diffi-

culty, arising as they do from the two natures
claimed by her who is one, correspond exactly to the
three temptations recorded of Christ in the outset
of His ministry — Christ who, it is also claimed,
was one Person with two natures. And, as a mark
of the Divinity of both Christ and His Church,
we noticed how such temptations can only really be
acute and continuous where the Personality tempted
is Divine as well as human.

4. Next we considered, in the public ministry of
Christ and the Church, first the manner of teaching
and then the substance of it. And we saw that the
marks of authoritativeness and a kind of imperious-
ness were characteristic of both. " He spoke as
one having authority; and not as the Scribes," since
there is no room for schools of thought among the
disciples of a Divine Teacher, amongst those who
have received an objective revelation. Human
societies, whose ambition is to seek and to ask and
to knock, naturally must allow a great deal of latitude as to the direction in which to seek, the best
form of words for asking, and as to which doors
had best be knocked upon. But a Divine Society
which has found, and received; a Society which
has already passed through the Door by which
men come to the Father; a Society which holds
the keys of that door — in her there is but one
Way, one Faith and One Life. She too, then,

speaks with authority; she, too, develops, and in certain departments even modifies that which was said " by them of old time." She alone proclaims, as through a trumpet, " I say unto you "; and she alone therefore is really obeyed by her children. We noticed also, in passing, that the same doctrines of Christ which aroused the sharpest opposition in His day rouse the sharpest opposition in our own — the sacramental system; Absolution; the Real Presence; and the claim to Divinity. To each announcement the same *bourgeois* question comes back, " Who can? — How can — this thing be ? "— a characteristic form of objection from those who think they know everything. " The thing does not fit in with my experience. Therefore it cannot be true."

5. Next we considered the question of Miracles; and we saw that their appeal lay primarily to those who were already morally disposed to believe; that practically no miracle can convince those who are determined not to believe; and that Christians are absolutely justified, considering the evidence already at their disposal, in regarding the miracles both of their Divine Master, and of their Divine Mother, as further evidences and proofs of the supernatural power at work behind them.

These then have been our subjects so far. In each case I have attempted to show that the characteristics of Christ as recorded in the Gospels are the characteristics of the Catholic Church and the Catholic Church only, in the fullest sense; that the effect of these characteristics upon the world is the same now as then; and that these characteristics cannot be reasonably explained except as belonging to an Unique and a Divine Personality.

PART III
PASSION AND REJECTION

I

GETHSEMANE

The whole of Nature exists on the principle of vicarious suffering; and to reject Christianity because of the doctrine of the Atonement is to reject Nature itself on the same account. To turn from Christianity in high-minded repudiation of the "injustice" of the dogmas of Pain as preached by her, and to seek peace and reassurance in the song of birds and the blossoming of flowers is, almost literally, to jump from the frying-pan into the fire. For the frying-pan at any rate stands for an attempt to use the fire intelligently, and the fire, unused, stands for mere destruction. Christianity at any rate suggests an endeavor to face facts and to interpret them; Nature offers the same facts without any interpretation. The shrike crucifies his food alive; flowers bloom on corruption; robins kill their parents; all life comes with birth-pangs, and exists only on terms of death. Man feeds on beasts; beasts on herbs; and herbs on minerals. These are facts, whether we like them or not. And Christianity at any rate encourages us to face them, and to say that minerals, by destruction, pass up into herb-life; herb-life into animal; animal into human. Christianity goes even further and completes the cycle by giving us reason to believe that man, by suffering, becomes elevated, and rises even to be "partaker of the Divine Nature" from whom all proceeds. If then these facts are contrary to our ideas of justice, we had better correct our ideas of justice, for they are simply untrue to life — whether of Religion or Nature.

In every world-religion,[1] therefore, vicarious suffering plays a prominent part. No religion which does not in some manner deal with that which is the very principle of the universe as we know it, can possibly command for long any important proportion of the human race.[2] A religion which does not recognize Pain as a redeeming or satisfying power is simply untrue to life and experience. Through the Old Law, therefore, sacrifice ran like a scarlet thread. In supernatural relations, as in natural, bulls and goats must die if man is to live. But it is reserved as the supreme and unique achievement of Christianity to recognize that the pain of

[1] As a rough definition of a "world-religion" I suggest, A religion that has numbered among its adherents at least a hundred million persons for a period of at least a thousand years.

[2] It is significant that Protestantism, as one of its main negations, rejected the Sacrifice of the Altar; and that Protestantism as a system is crumbling away.

Creation must involve the pain of the Creator — (since Love, and not mere force, is the mainspring of all life) — and to understand that God Himself out of His own Self-compelling Love becomes a Lamb in order that He may die for the lost sheep — that "the Son of God became a Son of Man, in order that the sons of men may become Sons of God"; that the Son of God dies that the sons of men may live.

We have seen how Jesus Christ lives in His Church; we have further to see how He dies in His Church. And first it is necessary to remember that Pain is not laid upon Him as upon an unwilling or unintelligent Victim; but how, before suffering externally, He stretches out His Hands to receive it — how He welcomes and takes down into the depths of His being, that He may first embrace it with His Will, that very pain by which He is to redeem the world.

In the Catholic Church this recognition of the principle of Pain is evident enough.

1. There are first the ordinary sorrows of the inner life in general.

Amongst non-Catholics pain is something of a puzzle. Non-Catholics usually seem to think that whatever else religion may fail to do for them, at least it must not fail to make them feel happy. If a man renounces the pleasures of sin, and accepts

9

the limitations and restrictions of the Divine Law, he demands at least that his religious emotions shall compensate and console him.   But amongst Catholics it is a commonplace — and especially amongst Catholic mystics[1] — that the Spirit of God is a sword that enters into the very deepest parts of the interior life; that desolations of soul, an agonized conscience, " dark nights of the soul," and the rest, are as normal accompaniments of true progress as are the exterior inconveniences and sorrows that greet the beginner.

Amongst the contemplative orders all this is, of course, the main part of their regular business. They go apart from the world, not, as shallow self-seekers seem to think, in order to escape Pain, but in order to seek it.   They are specialists in suffering — not merely in physical suffering — in weariness, in the scourge, the hair-shirt, the plank-bed — these are scarcely more than symbols — but in interior desolation, in " derelictions," in the loss of all consciousness of God, of all consolation and comfort, and above all in a sense of sin of which the world is simply unable even to form a conception.

2. Amongst Catholics alone, again, does it seem to be recognized that the sufferings of the individ-

---

[1] The mystics, it must be remembered, are not a " school of thought " in the Church.   They are only those who see a little deeper than others into the dogmas which they hold in common with, and in the same sense as, other Catholics.

ual benefit the world as a whole; that is to say, that
the Pain-principle of Nature is a principle of Grace.
If the Carthusian went into his cloister *merely* in
order to save his soul, there would be something in
the sneer of " selfishness " with which he is always
assailed. For non-Catholics — as a rule (and
quite naturally)— seem to be unable to regard
themselves as anything but detached units, each
wholly self-contained and self-seeking. They are
entirely without any glimpse of the vision of the
Body of Christ, that vast supernatural organism in
which the Lamb of God mystically suffers always
— that organism in which the agony of one member draws off the poison from the rest — that organism of which the most honorable members are
those in which Gethsemane manifests itself continually.

This principle, then, runs through the whole of
the Catholic Church from head to foot. In her not
only is the exterior sacrifice of the Cross offered
without ceasing, in the august mystery of the altar
—(since what Christ did once He does always)—
in one mode; and, in another, in the exterior sufferings of her members; but the interior pains of
Gethsemane are similarly perpetuated. Every true
priest in the confessional knows something of the
sense of sin borne by him on behalf of the penitent
—" I weep." sobbed the Curé d'Ars, " because you

do not weep"; every well-instructed Catholic knows how to offer his own sorrow for the sake of another soul; for in the Catholic Church alone is manifested that Nation of Priests of whom the first Pope writes;[1] for in the Catholic Church alone is that vast principle of vicarious Pain welcomed, recognized and used, on which the whole chain of life, even in the physical order, hangs together.

3. We have then, in all this, one more amazingly vivid sign of the identity of Christ and His Church. Each alike may use the same words; or, rather it is He Himself who, under two modes, uses the same words: "All ye that pass by, behold and see if there be any sorrow like to My sorrow!" "Here in My Church, and here alone, I reënact to the full, willingly and intelligently, that agony recorded of Me in the Gospels. Here, in the cell of the Contemplative, in the confessional of the worthy priest, in the bedroom of the selfless sufferer—in every interior agony bravely borne, I once more lie in the garden, bathed in blood, torn from Me, not by scourges, but by grief. Here, in the torturing sense of sin, borne by the innocent, once more the Prince of this world manifests His coming, though He finds nothing in Me; here, in every interior desolation, in the loss of friends accepted for the Great Friend's sake, in

[1] 1 Pet. ii. 9.

the lack of sympathy acquiesced in for the Great Love's sake — in all the loneliness, the misery of isolation, the silence, and the fierce resistance of the flesh against the spirit that holds it in check, is once more reënacted the tragedy of the garden of long ago. See how My Diaconate of Three lies sleeping for sorrow, a stone's throw away, and my Subdiaconate of eight at the garden door; while I lie here, alone and misunderstood, suffering that interior Passion of the Soul of which the exterior Passion of the Body is scarcely more than a shadow and a symbol. Here, in the Catholic Church alone is the agony of Gethsemane understood and felt, for in the Catholic Church alone is it willingly and deliberately planned and welcomed."

CHRIST'S FAILURE

We have compared the phenomena of the Gospels and the Church, and have attempted to see how they are not only similar, but identical; and we have just touched very lightly upon that peculiar attitude towards Pain which is characteristic of Jesus Christ, and characteristic also, and only, of the Catholic Church. For the Catholic Church alone amongst religious bodies welcomes and wills her own pain — (as is shown in her fruitfulness with regard to contemplatives and her organization of their life) — not only for the sake of the individual who suffers, but of the whole body to which he belongs.

The Church alone, I have said, recognizes and uses the principle. She is therefore accused of "morbidity" by those who resent the facing of Facts, and who believe that Pain is incompatible with Joy. But it is a singular misuse of a word. Morbidity is the state of unhappiness in a man who ought to be happy; while the Contemplative is a man who is happy when he ought, in the world's opinion, to

be unhappy. The moment a soul recognizes that
there may be a Joy in Pain which is absent from
Pleasure, she has taken the first step towards the
practical solution of the Problem of Pain.

So far, however, we have only discussed the
Church's interior attitude towards pain; later we
shall consider exterior pain, its meaning and its
functions. In the meantime it will be worth while
to reflect upon ·the characters of those who were
chiefly instrumental in bringing that exterior pain
to bear upon Jesus Christ, and to see whether they
do not correspond very closely with the characters
of those who in all times are the enemies and judges
of Catholicism. And it will be my endeavor to
show that the types persist to-day in a very significant manner amongst those who reject the claims
of the Church; that the kind of opposition aroused
by Him, is aroused by her, and that the same element of tragedy marks the progress of the Church
as marked His. And, so far as I may succeed in
showing that it is the Divine only that is so rejected, that no human theories arouse the same kind
of opposition — in other words that the type of
opposition aroused by the Church is unique in kind
as in vehemence — I shall also have succeeded in
showing that the Church has the right to make those
unique claims which she does actually make. In
the last two or three chapters I shall endeavor to

show that, great as is the tragic failure of the
Church, the triumph she ultimately elicits from it
is proportionately great, and greater; and that the
phenomenon of a continually recurring Resurrection from a death more than ordinary, is the supreme sign of her Divinity.

Let us begin by a few considerations upon her
" failure " in general, before passing on to a discussion of the kinds of characters to whom she fails
to appeal.

That the Church is in one sense the greatest
failure that the world has ever seen, is an obvious
fact, from the very magnitude of her claims and
the apparent smallness of her achievements.   Not
only does she not convert the hostile world as, it
would seem, she ought to do if she were Divine, but
she cannot even keep her friends faithful.   Whole
districts, countries and races that were once her
lovers are no longer so.   She failed, comparatively
early, to keep North Africa, once wholly her own;
she has failed within recent times in keeping France,
once her eldest daughter in Europe.   To descend
to particulars, in the districts of England where
she reigned supreme, almost within living memory
— in Cornwall, and parts of Scotland and Wales,
she has now almost more bitter enemies than anywhere else in the country.   Families that retained
the Faith through all the period of persecution and

ostracism have lost it in the rising tide of tolerance and peace.

Two main charges are brought against her by intelligent persons, as reasons for her failure.

1. First, that she does not move sufficiently with the times. It is an age, we are told, of material and social progress, of increasing knowledge, and of consequent modification of past theories. More and more, we are informed, the center of interest is coming to lie in this world; the next is, comparatively speaking, an unknown thing. Duties lie ready to our hands here — obvious and plain duties; and, if the Church would but give up her dreaming and her visions and occupy herself with practical matters, she might yet lead the armies of progress. But no! She is wedded to the past; she is too spiritual to live; she still babbles on about Heaven and Hell; she walks with her head among the stars. She is as much out of place as a hermit in a High-street. We do not want skin-clad prophets any longer; we want men of action and common sense.

2. The second charge brought against her is exactly the reverse of this. The Church, we are told, is far too worldly to be successful. Is it not a fact that the Jesuits — or at any rate Catholics — are at the bottom of all the sedition and troubles that the world has seen? They always will mix themselves up with what is not their affair! If

only the Pope, for instance, would dissolve his diplomatic service, and give up his claim to temporal power, and live as a simple paternal old man, busying himself with his own proper affairs, being content to direct the spiritual lives of his children, instead of attempting to interfere in the counsels of Kings — the Church might perhaps win back the respect she has lost. She is too much of a worldly sovereign to be the Representative of Him who said, " My Kingdom is not of this world."

The Church then is too much of a Prophet for practical men; and too much of a Queen and a worldling for the rest.

And in these two charges — brought against her continually — the world, amazing as it seems —appears to find no inconsistency!

When we turn to the Gospels, we find that it was exactly upon these two charges that Jesus Christ was condemned to death. If only He had taken the advice of either set of His friends, His life would not have ended in the appalling catastrophe of Calvary.

There was a time when His enthusiastic followers would have taken Him by force and made Him a King. Humanly speaking, if He had but grasped that offer, He might well have been able to march an army into Jerusalem, dethrone Pilate, seat Himself in his place and win at least a temporary monarchy. Yet He chose this very moment to hide Himself, to go back to the mountains and reassume the guise of a Prophet.

A little later He did directly encourage the idea. He deliberately caused a procession to be organized; He took His seat upon a beast provided for Him, and rode into Jerusalem with practically royal honors; the air rent with acclamations hailing Him as the Son of David on the way to His Father's city. And this too was a mistake, it seemed. He set all spiritually minded men against Him. "Master," expostulated the Doctors of the Law, "bid Thy disciples that they hold their peace." If, even then, He had taken their advice, and repudiated all temporal allegiance, He might quite conceivably have won a real spiritual homage instead.

Finally, it was on these two counts that He was arraigned and sentenced to death. Caiphas condemned Him because He claimed an emphatic Divinity. "By our Law He ought to die, because He made Himself the Son of God"— because He claimed a Kingdom not of this world. Pilate condemned Him because He claimed so emphatic an Humanity, because He claimed a Kingdom that was of this world. "Whosoever maketh Himself a King, speaketh against Cæsar."

The coincidence, I think, is more than remarkable. It is the Catholic Church, and she only, among all the denominations of Christendom that is at once too worldly and too other-worldly to be tolerated. The kind of religion that the world likes is a religion that is neither one thing nor the other — a religion that is not too vivid or eloquent about the next world, and not too practical about this — a gentle and pleasant compromise between the two — in a word: "Morality touched with emotion." This kind of religion is always successful, always at least tolerated. Such a religion as this never tramps to any Calvary; is never crucified between two thieves.

Now is it not eminently characteristic of Divine Truth, as distinguished from human opinion, that it should always and everywhere live in an atmosphere of tragedy? Is it not characteristic of Divine Truth, as distinguished from human opinion, that it should always be accused of being extreme in both directions at once? For Divine Truth always must be extreme — it must, so to speak, always overlap at both ends, just because it is Divine, and therefore much too big for this world. It must always be more human than man, and therefore be thought inhuman; and also a great deal more Divine than man, and therefore thought visionary and fantastic. A butterfly, if it had a mind, might think the human creature a very unpractical kind of phenomenon. He actually picks the flowers —

a brutal and uneconomical action, since they hold honey; the only thing the butterfly thinks worth considering — at one moment; and pays no attention at all to them at the next moment. So the world, terribly intent upon its own business, thinks the Church quite hopelessly inconsistent. The Church seizes money and jewels and architecture and music at one moment, busies herself in politics, in monarchies, and republics — in fact all those things that the world most values; and the next tells us that all these are of absolutely no importance — lets them all go, as recently in France — compared with the world that is to come. She is too intensely worldly to be truly spiritual; she is too intensely spiritual to be of any use to poor commonplace man. And because in this instance the butterfly happens to be the stronger, the Divine Man is nailed up, thorn-crowned, to the nearest tree; because He is too extreme, at both ends at once, for the eminently common-sense butterfly. He is fit neither for Heaven nor earth; therefore He is hung up between them.

But human societies do very well. No one wishes to crucify other denominations, simply because they consent to compromise in some form or another. They do "come down from the Cross" and save themselves in an attempt to save others. They do not understand that they cannot save both; and therefore the human race is content to tolerate them because they are so comfortably human. Is not this literally true? Is it not a fact that the average English family bears with complete equanimity the passing of its members from one denomination to another, or even to no denomination at all; but if a son or daughter becomes a Catholic, the two thieves are the only persons who ought to associate with them in future? . . . Certainly the Church has failed remarkably! But, then, so did Jesus Christ.

III

JUDAS

In the last chapter we considered generally the "failure" of Christ and of His Church; and Judas Iscariot is therefore logically, as well as historically, the first personage of the Passion to be considered. For, while his motives in detail, in their complexity and interaction, are unknown to us, one thing is certain — viz., that not only was he the one failure amongst the friends of Christ, but that the main reason for his apostasy, as for all true apostasies, was that Christ had failed to satisfy him. He had once believed, he had once been ardent and whole-hearted; children had blessed him as he came preaching the Kingdom of God with power, devils had been subject to him; and now, for some reason or another he had changed his ideals. That was all.

The Catholic Church has, I think, this characteristic in an almost unique degree, that while on one side she is capable of arousing the most passionate devotion that can ever be given to a Society, she also arouses, in those who leave her, the most violent opposition. An indifferent apostate is a very rare phenomenon. When persons leave other denominations they do not immediately turn round and assail them. I have known innumerable converts from very many forms of Christianity, as well as from agnosticism and positive infidelity; but it is exceedingly seldom that I have ever heard anything but expressions of affection or respect for the systems, or at any rate the persons whom they have left. The utmost I have heard is a certain impatient irritability or contempt towards the system, for having so long detained them on the road to Jerusalem, for having persuaded them that they were already members of a Divine Society, whereas now they see it to be but human after all. But if one wishes to hear reviling carried to a fine art, to hear an entire range of abusive vocabulary poured out, the meanest motives attributed, the worst interpretations put upon innocent actions, and all with the ardor of an ecstatic, one must turn to the apostate monk or the " escaped nun." The very intensity with which the Church is assailed by those who were once her friends, and the lengths to which they will go — this is as much a mark of what she is as is all the sanctity of her saints. Ex-Anglicans are often bored by the subject of Anglicanism, but they never treat it with fury or cynicism. Ex-Catholics, however, can seldom leave Catholicism alone. Judas does not become a critic, he does not even become a Pharisee; he becomes a supereminent traitor, just because of the supereminence of the Person he once adored. Of course these ex-lovers of the Church found their accusations again and again upon what is objectively true. They know well her weakest lines of defense, and her very human Humanity; they have a private key to the door of the garden where she may always be found. It is quite true that Christ did say something very like —" I will destroy this Temple, and in three days raise it up." It only required the transposition of a word or two to turn His phrase into the threat of a dangerous fanatic. And Judas could, no doubt, have supplied incident after incident witnessed by himself, countless words dropped in conversations by the wayside, to justify him in his betrayal of his Master.

1. Now, it is characteristic of Divine Truth alone to be treated in such a manner, always and consistently. Human opinions are as incapable of calling out this white-hot antagonism, as they are incapable of drawing out the highest devotion. The really monumental crimes of human history are always concerned with really great principles; and the very preëminence of Judas' treachery is a sort of witness to the unique cause which it concerned. The whole world consents that the crime of Judas is

the crime *par excellence* of human experience.   Is
not this very consent a witness to the unique character of the cause and the Person that were betrayed?   Other traitors have betrayed other friends,
but their names have not passed into proverbs in
consequence.

2. Next it is necessary to notice that without Judas, humanly speaking, the tragedy of Calvary would
have been impossible.   The mob had held Christ in
its hands before now, and had lost Him again; the
soldiers had come out against Him, and had re-
turned without Him; the Pharisees had sought to
entrap Him in His talk, without effect.   It needed
a friend to betray Him.   He does not escape from
those hands to whose loyalty He has committed
Himself.   Therefore on Judas alone is the final sentence pronounced.   Pilate, Herod, and Caiphas
still await the publication of their final sentence;
but of Judas the Judge has spoken judicially.   " It
had been good for that man if he had never been
born."

3. It must be noticed that the sin of Judas is,
from its very nature, a sin that can only, in its
full horror, be consummated by Christ's intimates.
It is the habit of Christians to treat it as a practical
impossibility for themselves.   " Is thy servant a dog
that he should do this thing? "   But it is a sin that
the " dog "— the mere attached dependent — cannot

commit. It is reserved, in its full luxuriance and malice, for the closest and warmest lovers of Jesus Christ — for those who have a kind of right to kiss Him and call Him friend.

The scandals of Catholic life, therefore, are just one more mark of identity between Christ and His Church. This or that Pope, bishop, nun, priest, or layman, whose names are quoted as bywords for sin, who are supposed to stand for unanswerable arguments against the Church's claim, are, so far as they are preëminent among sinners, also preëminent as Catholic credentials. A bad Catholic, it is universally acknowledged, is the foulest thing on God's earth; a corrupt pagan cannot be one-tenth as corrupt, simply because the same character that is capable of being raised to friendship with Christ, is capable also of the extremest enmity.

4. Neither is this sin of Judas so rare as is sometimes thought. In its full malice no doubt it is rare, but in some degree it forms an element in every sin against light.

(*a*) First come the Apostates proper — those who have deliberately (or even unconsciously as regards the full significance of each separate step of the process) changed their ideals, and have declared that change to the world — those who once hung upon the Church's lips, gave her love and loyalty, spoke in her name, and worshiped at her side, and who have gone out from the table of the Lord when the eternal night had fallen on their souls. *"Nox erat qui abiit,"* says St. Augustine. "He was night who went out." And it is those, primarily and pre-eminently, who turn Christ's triumph into failure. Remove, in imagination, all apostates from history, and nine-tenths of Christ's mystical Passion would be gone. *"Et tu, Brute!"* screamed Cæsar. "Friend, wherefore art thou come?" whispered Jesus Christ.

(*b*) Next come those who have changed their ideals without declaring it; who have retained, maybe, their faith, but not their love; who conform and speak and are silent, as Catholics; who even "believe" with an assent of the intellect, or the assent of emotion; but whose will-energy is else-where. These are those who in another manner, yet no less surely, betray Christ's Cause; it is of these that the world says in astonishment—"Is that man a Catholic?"

(*c*) And, finally, come those of every class of sinners, in whom the tragedy of betrayal is wrought in silence — those amongst whom stands every sin-ner, in however small a degree. For each soul is as great as the world, and in each soul there is room for all the tragedies of the world to be reënacted, as ev-ery puddle is great enough to hold the sun. For to each soul Christ comes, all trusting as a friend, and

in each soul He is betrayed over and over again,
into the cowardly hands of Pilate, and the grasping
hands of Caiphas, or to Herod's noisy self-love.
There He comes as to a garden to meet His friend;
and He is met indeed by that friend, and kissed.
. . . As every soldier carries in his knapsack a
marshal's baton; so every Christian carries on his
lips the possibility of a Judas kiss.

5. It is argued sometimes that the motive was
too little to account for Judas' sin; at least His
Master was worth more to him than thirty shillings!
Yet the same thing is done over and over again
at a smaller price than that. Over and over again
men will be found to sell their conscience — which
is to betray their Lord — for a moment's sensual
pleasure; or women for their social reputation or
a little empty self-love. It is all a matter of the
changing of ideals. If a soul lives long enough on
the plane of sensuality or of ambition, she finds
that Christ is worth less than nothing there. And,
above all, when once such a choice has been made,
how difficult is repentance! Remorse is easy
enough, but repentance means love; and a soul that
has lost her Lover has lost her own power of loving.

How helpless, then, seems the cause of Christ!
One degraded priest, one passionate or selfish child
has Him at his mercy, and betrays Him over and
over again. History is full of such sins, and, as

each sin is consummated, the cause seems lost.
Again and again Christ has been so betrayed, and
again and again the world has uttered its comment,
" He cannot keep His friends; He cannot save Himself.   Surely He cannot be the Son of God! "   Every apostate that has ever lived has been one more
incarnate argument against Him; every scandalous
Catholic life has furnished a thousand disproofs of
His Divinity, and yet Christ lives and is adored;
yet His Church with all the sins of her members
is accepted as Divine.   In fact, these betrayals are
worked up into the fabric of God's redemptive Plan.
" For the Son of Man must be betrayed into the
hands of sinners . . . and after three days He
shall rise again."   Can any Church be less than
Divine which has produced, and has survived, so
many Judases?

IV

We considered in the last chapter the preëminently Catholic sin of Judas — a sin of treachery. We must discuss now the opposition of the external world; for if the character of Christ's companions throws one light upon His Personality, the character of His enemies throws another, no less illuminating.

And first, *Caiphas*.

It is a remarkable thing, as I have pointed out before, that really religious opposition to the Church is at least as strong as any other. It is comparatively natural that the world, as world, should hate Catholicism, for, after all, the ideals of the two, as well as their methods, are completely different. The world, as world, wants one thing, and the Church, as Church, another. The world desires to be sufficient to itself, to round off its schemes, to complete itself in its own orbit. The Church tells us that that is impossible. As Mr. Chesterton has pointed out, it is not for nothing that the world is round, and that the Church is cruciform. For the circle, and still more the globe, is the very symbol

143

of completion and complacency; it suggests nothing
beyond itself; it cannot expand indefinitely without
bursting.   But the Cross is the symbol of absolutely
endless expansion; it is never content; it points forever and ever to four indefinitely receding points.
You can enlarge it eternally, without destroying its
figure.   It is perfectly natural, then, that the Ball
and the Cross should be in strong opposition.   But
what is remarkable is that certain kinds of religion
should be even more intensely antagonistic to the
Church.   I would far rather, as regards my own
comfort, visit the churches of Europe with an atheist than with an extremely fervent Protestant; for
the atheist, much as he may dislike my point of
view, has practically no common platform on which
he may abuse me and my co-religionists; we simply
have different ideals altogether.   I believe in God;
he does not.   Therefore there is nothing particular
to say.   We can walk together because we are so
entirely disagreed.   But the really fervent Protestant — the man, that is to say, who really believes
in Protestantism — thinks, at any rate, that he has
a great deal in common with me underneath; and
therefore there is no end to possible recrimination.
He tells me that I am quite right in believing in
God, but completely wrong in the kind of God that I
believe in.   Surely, he tells me, I cannot really believe that God likes incense and mumblings and

bowings and scrapings and the rest of it. Even if I travel with what is called a "tolerant" man, I find that there is always one thing after all that he cannot tolerate — from the nature of his own position — and that is my "intolerance." He can stand anything else, but not that. His very foundation is that all religions are pretty much the same in the long-run, and he has no words strong enough, therefore, for a religion which entirely denies that, that claims to be unique and final. The tolerant man, therefore, quite as much as the intolerant, must be, so far as he is fervent and sincere, the deadly enemy of Catholicism.

It is a very delicate and significant compliment, then, to the Catholic Church, that religious people are bound, if they are sincere and consistent, to hate her more than anything else in the wide world. Religious people may differ among themselves on every other imaginable point, but they are at any rate agreed on this, that the Church is the enemy and must be annihilated. You may do anything else, you may become anything else, and find forgiveness, but not if you become a Catholic. An eminent and very holy clergyman, known to me in England, once stated that he preferred his friends to commit any crime under the sun rather than that they should become Catholics. "Men repent," he said, "of murder and adultery; but they hardly ever repent of becoming Catholics." He was quite right. They do not.

Now, surely this is a remarkable phenomenon — that one religion, and one religion only, should have such a monopoly of being hated by religious persons. Anglicans do not hate Wesleyanism; Wesleyans do not hate Congregationalism; Congregationalists do not hate Christian Science. They disapprove, and they disagree, but their emotion is not vivid enough to be called Hatred. But they do hate Catholicism. There is no question about that. I am not aware that there are any newspapers in the world, for instance, whose main object is the destruction and discrediting of any sect under the sun; no newspaper primarily exists for the abuse of Anglicanism, or Presbyterianism, or Christian Science, or Swedenborgianism; but there are any number of newspapers in England, America, France, and Italy, whose main object is the abuse of Catholicism. Even the most diverse sections of Christianity will sink their differences and meet on a common platform in order to find fault with the Pope. Of course it is the fashion at the present moment, at least in England, to hide this hatred, and to pose as being tolerant even to Catholics; and we owe the abolition of the King's Declaration to that amiable assumption. Yet no one who knows England is really deceived into thinking it any more than a transitory pose. "Liberals" have been shamed at last into an attempt to be liberal. "Churchmen" have consented to an external act of justice to the Church. But conceive for one moment that liberty of conscience was really allowed in England and that the King did become a Catholic, and that the fact was made known — and it is absolutely certain that he could not continue to reign. And there is no other step that he could take which would cause such fury. Beneath all the fair words and the assurances of toleration, and the avowals of religious equality, there remains still, possibly only in the subconscious self of the country, yet certainly there, an hostility to Catholicism which is simply unrivaled with regard to any other form of religious belief. "Bloody Mary," or the Inquisition, or the massacre of St. Bartholomew are alleged as reasons for this hatred when it does make its appearance; but it is not really these things. It is Catholicism itself.

Turn now to the Gospels.

Caiphas and Annas were, without doubt, sincerely religious persons; they were, from one point of view, markedly unworldly. They were men who lived decent lives, who almost adored the Law of God, who had nothing whatever in common with the ideals of the Roman Empire as represented by Pilate. They hated to think that the Roman yoke lay on the shoulders of God's people; they resented in-

tensely the presence of the Roman garrison in the
Holy City; they, too, like the most fervent zealot,
looked for the Kingdom of God to come with power;
they "loved the beauty of God's house and the place
of the habitation of His glory." They were, in
short, convinced and pious Establishmentarians.
The one thing that Caiphas feared probably more
than death itself was the absorption of Israel in the
world — the coming of more Roman legions and
the taking away of what was left of the place and
the name of Israel. And therefore Caiphas crucified Christ.

"It is expedient," he said, "that one man should
die for the people; and that the whole nation perish
not." Now at first sight this seems a very extraordinary piece of reasoning. Why in the world did
he not try to win Jesus Christ over to his side, and
attempt to use the great influence that this Prophet
was beginning to command, for his own purposes?
They had so much in common after all; they both
loved the Law of God; they were both lovers of
holiness and purity and spirituality; they were both,
it seemed, "unworldly"; they both resented secular
interference in the things of the soul. There is
only one answer. Caiphas knew perfectly well, in
the bottom of his heart, that underneath all their
apparent agreement there was a fierce and irrecon-
cilable antagonism; that their ideals were not the

same; that Jesus Christ meant one thing by "the
Law of God" and himself another; that their whole
conceptions of even the character of God Himself
were different; and that there was not the faintest
chance or possibility of winning Jesus Christ over to
his side. It was unfortunate, but it was so. It is
true that there was no change of ideal in Caiphas,
as in Judas, and therefore the priest had the lesser
sin. Yet that there was divergence is evident
enough. So Caiphas went straight to the point,
with all the shrewdness of a real ecclesiastical states-
man. "Do you, or do you not, claim to be the
Son of God? Do you, or do you not, claim to be
unique? If you do not, we may yet come to terms.
If you will take your place with the rest of the
prophets, well and good. But if you claim to be
unique, there is no use in talking any further."
And Jesus answered, "I do." And the thing was
settled.

Now this, I venture to think, is the real quarrel
between Catholic and non-Catholic Christianity.
And it comes out at every point. It is the claim
to uniqueness that causes all the trouble. The Rit-
ualists would be friendly to-morrow if we would
but acknowledge the Branch or the Province theory,
and confess that they, too, were of one Church with
us; the Nonconformists would meet us with open
arms if we would but allow that "there are diversi-

ties of gifts but the same Spirit " (in the sense in which they understand the words), and that, while all were equally right together from our various points of view, we Catholics happened to have predilections for incense and ceremonial as a matter of temperament and individual taste. Even the Theosophists and the Neo-Buddhists and the Pragmatists and the " Modern-Thinkers " would be our cordial friends if we would but acknowledge that we were all striving for the same idea, in spite of our variations in dogma. Religious people would make up the quarrel to-morrow if the Church would but take her place with the rest. Religious people do, in fact, get on admirably with lukewarm Catholics who have learnt the trick of tolerant talking; who pretend that after all it does not matter so very much. But lukewarm Catholics are not the Church, and the religious world knows it. It is what is called " intolerance "— that is, the claim of the Church to be *the* Truth — that is at the bottom of the trouble; in short, what well-informed persons label as " Vaticanism " or " Ultramontanism." And so we see religious persons rending their garments in horror at this blasphemous arrogance; and we see Jesus in His Church, bound, spat upon and condemned, standing at the bar.

It is unnecessary to comment at length upon this. I have already touched upon the point more than

once. I would only urge a little steady reflection
upon the superb significance of the whole scene;
and that once more the question should be faced,
From whence does this amazing self-confidence and
self-consciousness on the part of Christ and His
Church really come, if it is not from above? What
is this mysterious influence which enables the Church
to resist the whole modern stream of "broadmind-
edness," and to stand out, like a rock, as the one
single religious body left in our midst which entirely refuses to rank itself with the rest? All other
denominations are prepared, at any rate at present,
to assume an attitude of humility, to make friends,
to allow that "the wider divergence is the deeper
unity," and all the rest of it. The Catholic Church
alone stands absolutely rigid, repeating her claim to
be the Truth, the whole Truth, and nothing but the
Truth; to be in need of no one, to be sufficient to
herself. And how is it that really religious persons,
who have so much, after all, in common with
Catholicism, yet are so fierce in its condemnation,
if it is not that they do subconsciously recognize
that their ideals are not the same — that themselves
are but human after all, and that this marred and
despised Figure, more than human?

V.

1. There is a certain type of character with which, I suppose, we all feel very great sympathy — I mean that type which refuses to class itself under any particular form of faith, but which has, underneath its professions of doubt and hesitation, a real sympathy with religion. It is religious in form, but not in (as I think) essence; or as itself would say, religious in essence, but not in form.

For example, a man of this type often calls himself an Agnostic. "Yes," he tells us, "I should very much like to believe as you do; but I cannot. It must be delightful to have a creed, and no qualms about it; to have sacraments in which you really believe; to feel confident that you really have got the truth in an adequate form, that you possess a Divine Teacher who cannot err. But I cannot possibly imagine myself taking up such a position. It is too simple to be true. I do not know what Truth is, but at any rate it must be larger than your little Church; it must be larger than any system. Whatever Truth — the Water of Life — may be, she cannot be so direct as this. Either she lives at the bottom of a very deep well, or she lives in the clouds. But she cannot possibly be so simple as to live in your little channels and pipes. No man in the world can possibly have the ,right to say, ' Come unto Me and drink.' " And it all sounds very large and wide and spiritual?

Sometimes this type of character changes abruptly into another. The Agnostic becomes a Gnostic — a Theosophist, let us say, or a Rosicrucian. Yet the spirit of the man is unchanged. He still maintains that Truth cannot possibly be *simple;* it must be remote and esoteric; a matter for the initiated, not for the vulgar. Truth is, to such a man, a mysterious recluse, dwelling within curtains, breathing in the atmosphere of flutes and ceremonies and red fire, shrouded in veils and trailing garments. She is not exterior, but interior. External religions are admirable for the mob, who are children and must be taught like children; but the real disciple must be an initiated adept, with knowledge beyond the ordinary. Truth is not simple; but he has found it.

Now to such a man as this, in whichever mood he may be, Catholicism cannot possibly be true. He has no very grave quarrel with it; he does not in the least wish to crucify it; only, he cannot believe it. It is too simple and common and direct. If he is

11

an Agnostic, he says it is too positive and too much systematized; if he is a Gnostic, he says it is not esoteric enough. How can that be Truth (with the largest capital letter) which is really accessible to the child and the Irish laborer?

Now this, as I read the Gospels, is precisely the spirit of *Pilate*. Obviously Pilate was a man of religious instincts. There are few judges on the bench to whom a wife would send the account of a dream she had just had. Certainly no wife would send such a message to her husband in court unless she knew that he had a certain weakness, at least, for the occult. His own behavior, too, his uneasiness, his reiterated questioning of Jesus Christ — all bear witness to his undoubted religious instincts.

Obviously, also, he had no sort of resentment against Jesus Christ; he did not in the least wish to crucify Him; in fact, he distinctly wished to release Him. He had a certain uneasy feeling about Him; but certainly it never entered his head for an instant that this figure could possibly be Incarnate Truth. Truth, surely, must be something quite different from this.

It is an extraordinarily pathetic scene. Here sits a man, obviously interested in Truth, or he would scarcely have asked a rhetorical question, so characteristic of the Agnostic of all ages that it has passed into a proverb: and here before him stands

One who was — so Catholics believe — the actual answer to his question. " What is Truth? " says Pilate. " I am the Truth," says Jesus Christ.

Now, this phenomenon is one that is being reproduced with extraordinary frequency in every age of history ; but perhaps never more than in our own.

" How charming it would be," says such an one, " if this Catholic religion really were true. But it cannot possibly be. It is too simple. How delightful to believe, like that priest in the pulpit, or this neighbor who sits beside me, that there is really and truly a Divine Teacher on earth, who is infallible, whose every word is absolutely true, whose guidance is unerring. But it is too simple and direct. No. Whatever Truth is it cannot be this. It cannot reside in this simple Figure standing patiently before the Judgment-seat of the world. Why, look at the kind of people she gathers round her, just a few children, some tired women, some laborers, some artists ; a few penitents who would give faith to anybody who gave them hope. Truth is larger and deeper than all this. I do not know what she is, nor her name nor her face ; but she cannot possibly be here."

Or we hear the Gnostic.

" Ah! if these Catholics only knew! How simple they are! How touching it all is! If they only knew the real secret of Truth ; if they could only see beyond the veil, as I do — if they could only understand that the truth is hidden, and must be hidden, from babes and sucklings, and revealed to the wise and initiated! But it is no good. So long as they actually believe that Truth dwells on broad steps in the light of day, with a yelling mob behind her, and a few broken-hearted friends sobbing in corners — it is no good talking. Why, look! This Truth of theirs actually has her arms tied behind her back; she is bloodstained and weary. Whoever heard of Truth in such a state as this! Truth is a splendid and majestic Queen, dwelling in inner palaces; not this broken caricature of a Queen, this mock-sovereign, with a reed-scepter and a crown of thorns. This is a mere popular parody of sovereign Truth — not herself. I have no quarrel with this poor thing; I would release her and let her go, if I had my way. How sad it all is!"

In a word, Pilate rejects Jesus Christ because He is too simple.

And yet the question rises, What do you expect God's Truth to be? If God be Truth, and God be Love, is it not absolutely inevitable that the Love of God should bring the Truth of God down to the level of the very simplest? Truth is at least as necessary for the simple as for the wise. Human opinion certainly must be as graduated as the human intellects which generate it: the wise will form

one opinion of the world, and the simple will form
another — if they are left to themselves. But if
they are not left to themselves —(and how can they
be, if God is Love?)— if they are not left to themselves, it must mean that Truth will be the same for
everyone, since Truth will be that which God reveals
to them. God's Truth, therefore, must always be
as Jesus before Pilate — must always be a Figure
fettered and bound by men's hands, bloodstained
with the struggle, and yet standing in the plain light
of day, equally visible to all, since He is sent to all.

Oh! these superior persons who ask, What is
Truth! They are the people who mistake vague-
ness for spirituality — as if spirit were not infinitely
more concrete than tables and chairs: they are the
people who are eternally asking, What is Truth?
and never answering their own question; the people
who think that seeking is nobler than finding, and
that the best thing to do after having knocked at a
door is to run away for fear it should be opened,
and something, perhaps unwelcome, look out. They
are the people who are so exquisitely subtle that
they never can see the obvious — persons who, as
has been said, are like a door so large that little people cannot go through it.

They are aware that God is infinitely mysterious
— that " God is a spirit "; but who are not aware
that " The Word was made Flesh and dwells

amongst us "— they think that co-relatives are con-
tradictions; that what is spiritual cannot be incarnate; and are unaware that the sole reason for the
existence of flesh is that spirit may express itself
in its terms.   They are always crying the versicle
of " Verily Thou art a God that hidest Thyself ";
and never answering it with its proper response,
" The Word was made Flesh and tabernacled
amongst us, and we beheld His glory."   They are
aware that God is mysterious; but unaware that He
must also be perfectly simple.   They think that the
" Living Bread," because it is Divine, cannot possibly
be given to children.

These people are always speaking of Modern
Thought and Progress.   They are forever talking
of the Spiritual Movements of the age — everything
to them is always new and epoch-making; they are
always wondering secretly what position they themselves will be considered to have won in the record
of religious thought.   They need not trouble; they
have already won an inalienable, and infinitely pathetic position, in the religious history of the world;
they actually, alone among all men, with the exception of Mary, are named expressly in the Christian Creed — so significant is their work —" Crucified under Pontius Pilate "!

And how wonderfully unconscious they are of
this one real claim of theirs to distinction!   They

are anxious about their significance in the religious movement of the time, and entirely fail to realize how actually vital they are to the consummation of the Divine Plan. Anatole France has somewhere a story of the later years of Pilate. He describes him, an old gray-haired man in his quiet villa, talking over with a comrade his experiences in Judæa.

"Was there not some trouble," asks his friend, "over a man called Christus? I forget the details; but I think he claimed to be one of the gods. I think you crucified him, did you not?"

Pilate sits a moment thinking over his wine-glass.

"No," he says presently. . . . "It may have been so. But I do not remember it."

VI

HEROD

In our last chapter we considered the Agnostics and the Gnostics — those who regard Truth as a recluse.

Let us turn now to their precise opposite. These persons we have been considering are those for whom the Truth is too simple: let us consider those for whom the Truth is too deep. But we need not spend long over them; they really are not worth it. Jesus Christ condescended to argue with Pilate, to speak to Caiphas and even to plead with Judas; but for Herod He had no answer but the dead silence of Divine scorn.

These Herodians fall into several classes: there are the cheerful noisy fools whose sole interest in religion lies in seeing something curious. We see them on the Continent a good deal — generally regarding High Mass through pince-nez and eyeglasses, and wondering on Palm Sunday whether really the priest is going to ride on a donkey or not. . . . Well, let them alone. Our Lord did.

But some of them are really more subtle than this.

There are, first of all, those who are perpetually asking for objective proofs that they can understand — who think that they have settled the Catholic religion once and for all when they have examined, let us say, some exaggerated story about Lourdes, and found that it will not bear investigation. Their view of religion is that unless it can produce extraordinary and startling results which can be verified in five minutes, it cannot be true. There is a school of psychologists which so treats religion, which takes the abnormal cases, the ecstasies, the apparitions, the levitations, and neglects the quiet piety of millions, the countless uneventful but heroic lives of simple faith and suffering, and thinks that it has really examined religion. " And when Herod saw Jesus, he was very glad; for . . . he hoped to see some miracle done by Him." The point of religion, to such persons, is its extraordinary and unusual side. They demand that the Creator should always be doing conjuring tricks instead of creating, and their only view of the Light of the World is that it should break out continually into fireworks.

A yet more subtle subdivision of the Herodians consists of those who are always demanding material statistics of a Spiritual Society. They are always comparing Catholic and Protestant countries to the discredit of the former. And the remarkable thing is that they appear to think that the object of the Catholic Church is, or ought to be, the production of well-fed and prosperous business men. They notice that the drains in Ireland are not all that they ought to be; that Spanish guns cannot shoot as straight as American guns; that Elizabethan England succeeded in killing more Indians and capturing more treasure-ships than the England of a century earlier; they think that colonial enterprise, and Consols, and Government stocks, and machinery are the fruits of the Spirit. They do not say anything at all about the purity of Ireland, or the holy family-life of Catholic Germany, or the fact that Catholic Spain still really worships God at a considerable expense of both time and money; or that what is left of Catholic France still does more for missionary enterprise than any other country in Europe; or that the number of communions made annually in the diocese of Cologne exceeds the number of all Anglican communions made in the British Isles — all those things, to them, are not religion. Religion must not be tested by Love, and Holiness, and Worship, and Faith, and Self-sacrifice — No: it must produce Commerce, and a high rate of interest, and State efficiency, and tram services and electric light.

Finally, the most religious Herodians of all conceive of religion as that which gives them agreeable sensations in what they believe to be their soul. Emotion is to them the mark of a standing or falling Church. They like incense, so they go to High Mass; they do not like Latin, so they stay away. One preacher makes them feel warm and happy, so they sit under him. Another makes them feel cold and unhappy, causes them to be uncomfortable — really uncomfortable, not pleasantly so — about their sins; and they do not hear him again.

These people, then, as a rule, conclude against the Catholic Church, because — in spite of the popular saying to the contrary — they ultimately find out that emotionalism is very much discounted in the Catholic Church; that there is very little glamour indeed after a month or two; and that she is distinguished for a terribly cold and businesslike way of dealing with the soul, insisting upon obedience rather than sacrifice, and fidelity and humility and duty, rather than upon incense and Sunday-evening sensations.

Now what is the Herodian mistake? It is this: The Truth is too deep for them.

When Christ stood before Herod, Herod wanted one thing, and Christ offered him another. Herod wanted his scepter to be duplicated, a man-at-arms to be struck dead and raised again to life — he wanted something to relieve the intolerable monot-

ony of a sensual life : he desired a new sensation, and
superficial signs — in short, fireworks. And He who
claimed to be the Light of the World offered him
light instead — the white flame, without flicker or
flare, of a Divine Personality in the lantern of a
Sacred Humanity.

Now, this is precisely the appeal of the Catholic
Church, as we have considered.   It is true that she
does miracles, or rather that He who dwells in her
does them, as He did two thousand years ago.   It is
true that He does do sensational things; He did
ride into Jerusalem on Palm Sunday; He still, as
Eternal Priest, offers mass in every Catholic church.
He does do useful works; He does feed multitudes
with bread; He does build up a wholesome domestic
life and a sound social system wherever his sover-
eignty is received; He does offer marvelous consolations; He truly comforts the penitent, and thrills
His lovers as they consummate their union with
Him at every altar-rail.   But, for all that, His real
fundamental appeal does not lie in these things.   It
lies in one thing only — the appeal of his whole
Personality to ours.   As he stood before Herod, that
appeal was eloquent, though there were no particular
sensations or proofs.   As He stands before the sen-
sation-mongering world to-day in that Church in
which He dwells, He makes the same appeal.

Religion is not a matter of mere emotion, any

more than of mere intellect. The man who says, " Unless I *feel,* I will not believe," is as narrow and foolish as the man who says, " Unless I understand, I will not believe." The Love of God can no more be compressed into a single human heart than the Wisdom of God into a single human mind. Mr. Balfour says somewhere that " if the scheme of Revelation were small enough for our intellectual capacity, it would not be great enough for our spiritual need." So, also, if the Love of God were reducible to our tiny emotional capacity, it would not have been great enough to have redeemed the world by giving the Son to death. Religion, then, is a great deal larger than brain or heart — than comprehension or feeling. It must at least touch the *will;* for however small our will may be, it is always large enough to be united to the Will of God.

Religion, then, is larger than any one department of our nature — it *must* be so, if it is Divine. It is the personality of the Catholic Church as a whole that appeals to the personality of man as a whole. God does not condemn us for not understanding, or for not feeling; but He does condemn us for not adhering to Him. He places His personality, dwelling in His Church, at the bar of our personality; and the sentence we pronounce on Him is the sentence He ultimately pronounces upon us.

Still, as of old,
Men by themselves are priced.
For thirty pieces Judas sold
Himself, not Christ.

This, then, is Herod's crime in every age — not that he asks for miracles, but that he asks for nothing else; that he has so lived in sensation and externalism that all his personality has run to seed; he lives only in sensation; he is not a complete man at all.   He is as a man who can only read his news in headlines.

"There are plenty of people," said an Irishman in Boston the other day —" plenty of people who are dead without knowing it."   "Yes," said his friend, "only they haven't the sense to lie down."

And this is Herod's crime now.   He is dead without knowing it.   He has missed the point of Life, and thinks it to lie in sensation.   He sees nothing in the Catholic Church except her claim to work wonders; she is to him only a beneficent Society, or a police force, or an artistic corporation; and if she fails, in his opinion, in any of these functions, she no longer is of any interest to him.   She can only be laughed at and made game of.   So Herod had his sensation out of Jesus Christ after all.   He dressed Him up as a sham King; he laughed loud and long with his men-at-arms, and sent his God to death.   We all win from God exactly what we deserve.   We all get from God exactly what we really want of Him.

VII

We must pass on to the final scene. In previous chapters we have considered various personages who sent Jesus Christ to Calvary. Let us now consider His journey there.

We have observed how what is called "current religious thought" always condemns Christ just because it is "current," and not fixed; how for one section of humanity Christ is too simple, for another too deep. Let us look at the whole thing once more from another angle.

There are three great ideals in the world — summed up under the three well-worn words, the Good, the True, and the Beautiful. People are always talking about these things under various disguises; but they cannot escape from the fact that, if ultimately analyzed, their ideals always fall under these three heads. For all energetic Society is made up of three elements — those who devote themselves to Law and Order and Social Reform and ethical and civic virtues, and so forth — what may be called the Good — all those things that people attempt to enforce by, and incarnate in, regulations and rules and Law.   Secondly, those who are always pursuing ideas of a final kind, schemes of the universe, cosmic explanations, philosophy — in a word, Religion, or Truth.   Thirdly, the artists of every description — those who live for something between the Good and True, something that partakes of the nature of both, and yet which is neither; who live for sensation, and feeling and delicate fancy, and thought that is valued because it is exquisite, rather than because it is true, because it feels good rather than because it necessarily is good — in a word, the Beautiful.

Now each of these sections of the world condemns Catholicism.

1. The seekers after Law condemn it because it seems to them lawless.   Catholicism appears to them the one disturbing element in Society.   They themselves, as I have pointed out already, endeavor to round off this world in itself, to make Society sufficient to itself to organize Society apart from God. They condemn Catholicism, therefore, because Catholicism is always appealing to another world, declaring that all this is only a detached fragment, a broken arc, that it must be remembered, in all schemes of restoration, that temporal existence is but a part of Another Whole.   Again, Catholicism is always urging that men are warped by original sin, that external interference is absolutely neces-

sary if the world is to be healed — in short, that
Redemption from outside is demanded.   The Law-
seekers claim that man is risen and rising — not
fallen.

Or put it in another very concrete way.   These
Law-supporters are always finding that the trouble
in the world is caused by Catholics (and they are
more right than they know).   Most of the great
cataclysms of history are caused by Catholics — the
massacre of St. Bartholomew, the Inquisition, the
Spanish Armada; these never would have happened
except for Catholicism.   And each of these things,
and many like them, if you analyze them far enough,
arise from this appeal — often perhaps a misapplied
appeal — to the Supernatural, which is the very life
of Catholicism.   The massacre and the Inquisition
both arose from the Catholic claim that God's Truth
was more important than men's bodily comfort.
The Armada was inspired by the idea that Catholic
unity — the Commonwealth of God on earth — was
a greater thing than England's National Independence.   So again and again in history it is this Catholic appeal to a supernatural idea — rightly or
wrongly conceived — that is at the bottom of sedition and trouble: from the broken peace of the
Roman Empire in the province of Pliny, and of
Elizabethan England, down to the most recent
estrangement of father and son in a home where

12

Catholicism has found entrance.   With one consent
the great Law-givers and Law-supporters of the
world condemn the Catholic Church as the enemy
of real peace and order.   Caiphas and Pilate are
quite agreed upon this point, and quite rightly so
from their premises, even if upon nothing else.

2. Next, we have seen how Catholicism is condemned by all religious bodies whose main idea is
the pursuit of Truth rather than its possession —
to whom Truth is an ideal, rather than a series of
real and solid facts.   Christ is condemned by these
just because He is a living, breathing, and accessible
Personality, down on the world's stage, instead of
an abstraction at the bottom of a well, or an im-
personal Force beyond the stars.   Pilate condemns
Him for this, as well as for being seditious.   Herod
fails to understand Him for the opposite reason —
just because Christ's is too mighty a Personality
for Herod's nonentity to realize Him.   Both in
their way are seeking Truth.   For one it consists
in a sort of dream, for the other in a sensation.
The devotees of the True condemn the Truth no
less finally than the supporters of Law condemn
the Lawgiver.   Caiphas, as the representative of
Lawful Truth, National Religion, agrees with them.

3. Lastly, the artists condemn Him.   I am
aware that artists often seem not to do so — in
fact, in words they seek to praise Him, but it is

only on matters on which they do not understand Him. They love the crucifix of ivory and gold; but they hate the Living Crucifix of Calvary. It is far too real and sensational to do anything but repel those who live by mere symbolism. The blood is too red, the wounds too wide, the face too deathly; above all, the lights are too low for the colors to be appreciated. Their praise is not sincere, or at any rate not genuine. How can those who speak of Art for Art's sake, love Him who teaches that all must be done for God's sake? How can those who live for exquisite and satisfactory sensation understand the cry, "I thirst"? How can those who confess openly that they truly live only when they feel, sympathize with Him who in the very climax of His earthly life cried, "My God, my God, why hast Thou forsaken Me?"

Artists then — the pursuers of the Beautiful simply for the sake of the Beautiful, and not for His sake who is Absolute Beauty, and therefore also content to be marred and disfigured for the sake of the unbeautiful — artists when they are really sincere, or rather, let us say, when they really understand the Church with her terrific teaching on the eternal hideousness of sin, and the duty of detachment and mortification and crucifixion — artists may now and then blurt out the truth — that the Church is not beautiful but ugly, that she is perpetually spoiling the joy of life by her monotonous prohibitions, Thou shalt not . . . Thou shalt not; that she is continually urging upon the world that which the world finds the most dreary of all things — its duty; and that it must resist the only thing it wishes to yield to — which is temptation; that she is always trying to substitute the bloodstained Christ for the vivid and lovely Apollo; that she provides the skeleton at every feast as well as in the cupboard; that she is the kill-joy of Creation, in spite of her Botticellis and her Raphaels and her Palestrinas. Swinburne in a few incomparable lines has uttered with the most superb passion this deep undying protest of the lovers of the Beautiful against the lovers of the Crucified:

Wilt thou yet take all, Galilean? but these thou shalt not take.
The laurel the palm and the pæan, the breasts of the nymphs in the brake,
And all the wings of the Loves; and all the joy before death . . .
Thou hast conquered, O pale Galilean; the world is grown gray with Thy breath.

Now, there are three great languages of civilization: Latin, Hebrew, and Greek.

Latin is the language of Law — the language of those old Romans, whose genius lay in law.

Hebrew, the language of religion: that in which

God spoke to His people; the language of those people who first dared to speak with God as a man with his friend.

And Greek, the language of the most superb artists that the world has ever seen.

The Good, the True, and the Beautiful.

Pilate, the supporter of Law, has cast Him off in the name of the Roman Empire and of the Roman peace which He has troubled.

Caiphas has rent his clothes, and repudiated Him who has blasphemed against the Truth.

And Herod, the lover of sensation, the builder of palaces, has dressed Him in a scarlet robe — (notice the touch of art, even there!) — and sent Him back to Pilate as a kill-joy, and a disappointing impostor. And for once Herod and Pilate are friends — the inartistic Law and lawless Art — friends in their common enmity to One who has refused to identify Himself with either.

"And Pilate wrote a title also. And the writing was, Jesus of Nazareth the King of the Jews: And it was written in Hebrew, in Greek, and in Latin."

Is it quite a meaningless coincidence that as Christ went on the Way of Sorrows, He bore about His neck a board on which his condemnation was written in the language of Law and Order, the language of Truth, and the language of Beauty?

Whether or no it was an insignificant detail then, it is certainly an exceedingly significant fact now. For it was in the name of the Good, the True, and the Beautiful that He was condemned; and it is in these same three names that He is driven now, incarnate in His Mystical Body, along that eternal Way of Sorrows that we call human history. On every side rise up the condemning voices against Her who claims the allegiance of the world that has cast her out.

"The Church," cries one, "is the enemy of Law, and Society, and mutual toleration. She is the destroyer of the world's peace, since she points to a Peace that the world can neither give nor take away; the breaker up of all those pleasant compromises and relationships that make the world's machinery work smoothly. She is the eternal enemy of the Good, as we understand it. Crucify her in Latin!"

"The Church," cries another, "is the enemy of Truth; for she professes to have found it and to possess it. She is the enemy, therefore, of all sound education and research and science. She dares to claim to be the very Truth. How can that be, since we are not aware of it? True religion consists in searching and asking and knocking — never in finding. This alone is the Truth about God, that He hides Himself. The only, thing that we know about God is that He is Un-knowable. Then crucify her in the name of that God — in the name of all those religious socie-ties who are humble enough to confess that they are but human. Crucify her, then, in the name of that God who always speaks in clouds and dark-ness — but never in the light of day — the nega-tive God of Sinai who says, Thou shalt not, but never, on a Mount of Beatitudes, Thou shalt. Crucify her in Hebrew."

" The Church," cries the third, " is the enemy of all true Beauty. She dares to say that the beauty of this world is not absolute and final; that it may be a snare; that at the best it can be but a sacrament; that contrasts of good and evil are not artistic; that Art can never possibly exist for Art's sake; but only for God's sake, or man's. She is the preacher of mortification, and denial and self-repression. She dares to say that man's highest life does not consist in self-expression, but in self-sacrifice. Then take her at her word and let her die. Crucify her in the language of Apollo and the Muses. Crucify her in Greek!"

SUMMARY OF PREVIOUS CHAPTERS

Once more, before passing on, it will be well to sum up what has already been said, and to end with one or two final observations.

We have considered the element of tragedy — one might say the environment of tragedy in which Divine Truth must always find itself in the world. Human opinions and human schemes are always at home here, since the world is their native place; but Divine Truth, or Revelation, is always a stranger, and sooner or later will be treated like one. The extreme hatred and opposition, then, which our Lord aroused more than any living being has ever aroused it; and that same hatred and opposition which similarly mark the progress of the Church in which He lives, are very strong arguments indeed for His and her Divinity, for their transcendence of Humanity. In her willing acceptance of pain we saw how she identifies herself not only with Nature, but with the God of Nature — with God, that is, in a Garden — yet unhappy, not happy, in that Garden. As He went out to embrace grief, before she embraced Him, so the Church makes willing sacrifice (which is the practical solution of the problem of Pain) the very heart of her system: it is she and she only who organizes and directs the life of interior mortification. Others look to Religion for comfort and sensible sweetness. She alone dares to face and to incorporate into her life, as did Jesus Christ in Gethsemane, that amazing and redemptive principle of all creation,— that life only exists through death, and Joy through Sorrow.

Then we considered again the exterior opposition of the world, and saw how the witness of that to her Divinity is especially marked in the case of those who were once her friends. The resentment of the apostate is the bitterest resentment in the whole world. The crime of Judas is the most vivid and the most forcible crime in human history.

Next we considered Caiphas — the type of all religionists who hate Catholicism. At the bottom of their hearts, in spite of their professions of a common Christianity, they know perfectly well that the Catholic Church is entirely different from themselves; since she claims to be unique — to be the Teacher come from God, and not merely one of the prophets. They themselves, on the other hand, claim that religion is not the particular property of any sect: all have their rights; none has an exclusive right. Therefore they rend their garments in sincere horror in the face of this appalling claim, and condemn her to death.

Next we considered Pilate — the type of man for whom Catholicism is too simple; the man who is always asking, What is Truth? and never finding it. It is not that he has any hatred of Catholicism; on the contrary, he thinks it a harmless and rather beautiful and pathetic phase. But it certainly cannot be the Truth. So he is forced by circumstances, in spite of his personal sympathy, to condemn her to death.

Or else he is one who has found some little esoteric Society who worships truth all by itself, who thinks that truth is the prerogative of the initiate, or the philosopher, or what he delights to call "the thinking man or the Mystic." It cannot possibly be the possession of the vulgar. The fact that the common people believe anything is to him an absolute evidence that that thing is not true. Truth is never the possession of babes and sucklings: it is the pearl of great price shining only in the locked cupboards of the wise and prudent. It cannot possibly be the marble that children play with in the streets. That would be much too simple and too royal, as, too, are the golden streets in which they profess to play.

Then we considered the Herodians — those for whom the Truth is too deep. For these, truth must always be something sensational — either it must be abnormal, or it must produce solid statistics in terms of finance and commerce and municipal reforms and town halls; or it must be sensational in the strictest sense — that which makes people feel sentimental, or comfortable, or devout and pleasantly regretful. It is not to these a

Solid Fact, true whether they like it or not. It must always justify itself to them in some superficial way. It must never say, I AM THAT I AM; but, I AM what you feel that I AM.

Then we looked at the Way of Sorrows from another angle altogether; and we saw how those who were always talking about the Good, the True, and the Beautiful, always crucified Christ each in his own appropriate terms. The pursuers of the Good — those who think simply of mutual human relationships, and therefore always adore the Law that adjusts those relationships and keeps the machine running — condemn Him as a Lawbreaker. The pursuers of the True — literally the pursuers, for it is an essential part of the process never to come up with their quarry — condemn Him in the sacred name of Religion — the name they give to this agelong search that never finds (in fact, one phase of Pilate over again). Finally, the artists condemn the real bloodstained Crucifix as a darkener of the sun, and an outrage on the fair name of Nature.

And so Christ is crucified, in Jerusalem and in every country of the world, in all the three languages of civilization. The Law-lovers, the Philosophers, and the Artists are agreed on this and this only; they are made friends together on this one point; those who otherwise are at enmity —

Pilate and Caiphas and Herod — those all with one consent cry altogether —" Let Him be crucified."

I will make but one observation to conclude.

Is it possible to believe that a Cause so unique in arousing opposition, so universally and eternally condemned, so provocative of the fury of all right-minded people — a Cause that is capable of being the central figure of a tragedy so terrific, and of a failure so gigantic — can be human in its origin and nature? If it were of the world, would the world, so concentratedly and so intensely, hate it, even to death and Crucifixion?

PART IV
FAILURE AND TRIUMPH

I

THE CROSS

We considered in the previous pages the manner in which Christ is rejected in the Gospels and in the Church; how every ideal which is not for Him, every ideal placed outside Him, is against Him. The followers of the Good tolerate the followers of the True; the Artists tolerate the Law-givers; but all are combined against Him. Herod and Pilate are made friends together. Caiphas and Pilate hold long consultations together, as soon as Christ appears on the scene. "The Kings of the earth stand up, and the rulers take counsel together. . . ."

Our first point to-day is the magnitude of the failure of Christ, in the Gospels and in the Church. Not only, as has been noticed before, does He not convince the world, but He cannot even keep his friends faithful. Peter, on whom the Church is built, denies Him; John, who lies on His breast at supper, is silent when this friend is accused.

There was never any failure so stupendous as that of Calvary.

In history it is precisely the same story, over and over again. It is possible for the enemies of the Church to point to period after period in history, and to show, with at any rate some reason on their side, that the failure of Catholicism is due to the failure of Catholics. "Your principles are splendid," they tell us; "at least they sound splendid. But why are they not put into practice? The Sermon on the Mount is an exquisite ideal, but why do you not try to realize it? What is the matter with Christianity is that there are no Christians. You are always making good beginnings, but you never live up to them. You were magnificent under Nero and Diocletian; but so soon as you seemed really to have conquered the world, you allowed the world to conquer you. You saved others; yourselves you cannot save. You were unworldly so long as Nero burnt and tortured you, but you became as worldly as everyone else so soon as Constantine tolerated you. You made a fine effort in the thirteenth century; you really produced some saints; but as soon as your Religious houses were built, they began to corrupt. You had glorious ideals when you began to Christianize Europe; but as soon as you Christianized it you began to become pagan again yourselves in the Renaissance.

Considered as a human Society you certainly are a success, you have astonishing vitality and energy; but as a Divine Society, which you claim to be, you are an amazing failure."

Now, this is precisely the story of the Gospels. Again and again there came moments when the success of Jesus Christ seemed almost assured. There were moments when the whole world went after Him who seemed so perfectly to meet its ideals; when the world itself would come and take Him by force and make Him a King; when the kingdoms of the world seemed laid at His feet; and yet, somehow or another, it all came to nothing. His whole life on earth was a kind of crescendo of popularity, up to the last moment; and then, in an instant, it all crumbled down again to nothing. Palm Sunday immediately preceded Good Friday. The procession of one was almost a replica of the procession of the other. There were a few details different; the spear-shaped palm leaves became palm-shaped spears; but the crowd was the same, the cries were the same, acclaiming the King of the Jews; the central Figure was the same. But the triumph turned to failure so soon as His central claim was made. He was welcomed and honored as a mere earthly King; He was rejected and condemned as a Heavenly King. Humanly considered He was something of a success; Divinely considered He was a failure.   As a demagogue He would have triumphed; as a God He was crucified.

Now, all this is very largely true.   We may regard the progress of Christ in the Gospels and in the Church as a triumph which fails, or as a failure which triumphs.   Non-Christians take the one view, and Christians the other.   It depends entirely on our standpoint — whether this world is our platform, or the next.

This, then, brings us right up face to face with the problem of Suffering and Failure.

1. This problem of Suffering is the one problem of all ages.   Every age produces a new solution. It was once thought, with extreme simplicity, that it was merely a matter of accurate reward and punishment —" Be virtuous; and you will be immune from suffering "— that God fought not with the largest battalions but with the most pious. And, again and again, the theory broke down. " In spite of my beautiful theories," cries David, " I see the wicked flourishing like green bay-trees. They come into no misfortune like other folk, neither are they plagued like other men.   Then thought I to understand this; but it was too hard for me.   Until "— but the rest comes later.

Or again, men have thought to solve the problem by suggesting that interior consolations always compensated for the exterior sufferings of the virtuous; that they really felt happy, in spite of appearances to the contrary. This lasted tolerably well as a theory until men really began to know their own souls; and then they found that interior sufferings were just as real, and even more poignant than exterior. They found, moreover, that it was actually the good who suffered in this way more than the bad; that the sensitive, delicate conscience and perceptions were tormented in a manner of which the superficial animal knew nothing; that suffering was not just a question of external scourge and nails, but of a Gethsemane agony so acute that the soul herself sweated blood. So they were driven from this stronghold too.

Finally, it has been suggested by one of the most recent and most prosperous of the American sects that the problem of pain is no problem, because there is no pain!

Now, I need hardly say that I do not propose to suggest another solution of my own; but I think it is worth while to point out the solution that Jesus Christ offers. His solution of suffering is to suffer.

Indeed, this is not so fatuous as it sounds, if it will be remembered that the intellect is only one department, and that a very small one, of our being. We noticed, when we considered Christ before Herod, that Herod's mistake was that he tried to compress the question before him into the single point of sensation or emotion. He did not judge Christ with the whole of his being, but with a part only. He condemned Him because He did not satisfy an arbitrary emotional test. Now, it is just as foolish to judge the problem of Pain by an intellectual test. If pain were a mere matter of intellect, it might be reasonable; but pain affects the whole of our personality at once — physical, mental, emotional and spiritual. Pain therefore, like Religion itself, is a thing that has to be judged by the whole of our personality. In a word, it has to be experienced; and somewhere in this total experience, not in any mere intellectual explanation, the solution lies.

Now this was the solution of Jesus Christ. " He learned obedience," says St. Paul, " by the things that He suffered." He solved pain by enduring it. He opened every fiber and nerve of His Human Nature to pain; there was no whole spot in Body or Soul. Physical and spiritual thirst were alike parts of His experience. " I thirst! . . . Why hast Thou forsaken Me? . . . My soul is athirst for the living God." He experienced solitude — the solitude of failure. " Of the people there was none with Me." " He came to His own and His own received Him not." He was obedient unto death: He tasted Death, and there-

fore He conquered it. But the great point of all
is that with His Will He did all these things. I
lay down my Life of Myself." He did not merely
bear the Cross; He took it up — first, interiorly in
Gethsemane; then exteriorly at the steps of the
Prætorium.

He did not, therefore, argue about pain; for you
can no more compress pain into mere argument
than you can compress Religion, or exactly analyze
Love. These really great things must be experienced; you have not all the data of the problem of
pain, until you have suffered all of it. And is it not,
after all, a solid fact, that it is not the sufferer who
is most perplexed by the problem of pain, but the
people who look on — in fact, the people who regard it merely intellectually? You can no more
solve the problem of pain by the intellect alone,
than you can explain the beauty of a sunlit sea
or the augustness of a thunderstorm by chemical
analysis of sun and sea-water and electricity. Men
do not say, " I will not believe a sonata by Bee-
thoven is beautiful unless I can smell it. I will
not consent that theft is a crime unless I can taste
it to be so." Yet people do have the effrontery
to say, " Unless I see I will not believe," or " Unless I understand I will not believe." Or, " Unless
I can intellectually apprehend the meaning of pain
I will not submit to it without a protest." The ac-

tual sufferer therefore, if only he will not try to
be too clever — which is another word for trying
to be narrow-minded — the actual sufferer is not
nearly so much puzzled by pain as his friend who
looks on; and the *willing* sufferer — he who actually coöperates with and welcomes pain — is not
puzzled at all. He cannot explain it: he cannot,
that is, throw the experiences of his whole personality into terms of a part of it; but he is no
longer puzzled. He knows. It is like a man in
love: he cannot put it into words; he bursts out
in sonnets, it may be, or serenades; he will talk
about it for hours together; but he will also end
by saying that words and music are no good, that
you must experience it to understand it. It is
much bigger than any analysis that can be made
of it. That is why lovers, and contemplative
monks who scourge themselves for joy, are considered the monumental fools of the world. It is
because they cannot put into words what is utterly
incapable of being put into words — because they
grow incoherent and ecstatic, as they are bound to
do — because they cannot translate into terms
which the poor, narrow-minded world seems to
think are the only terms worth using — because
they cannot write down with pen and ink — what
all the blood of the human heart cannot describe.
It needs the Blood of God, forced from Him in

Gethsemane, torn with scourges from Him in the Prætorium, sucked from Him by nails and thorns, and finally tapped by the spear, to its very last drops, from a Sacred Heart — it needs this Blood, offered willingly, adequately to experience and to show what is the solution of the problem of pain — *which is, in fact, the very same thing as the problem of Love.*

Now this, I think, very closely touches the point of Christ's agelong " Failure of the Cross." By the word " success " the world means intelligible success — success that can be expressed in terms of intellect, and therefore not at all wonderful, since we " wonder " only at that which we can apprehend, but cannot comprehend. And that is exactly the kind of success that, to one who understands that nothing except complete Personality is worth anything, is the kind that is not worth having. Divine success — a success, that is, that is larger than man's intellect, larger even than man's whole being — that must always appear paradoxical. It must, that is to say, be continual failure — a failure so complete that it ought to be the end of the enterprise, and yet not be the end of the enterprise. Its success must be expressed in terms of failure; as a sunlit sea, or lovelit eyes, must sometimes be expressed in terms of a black lead pencil. The Divine Cause must simultaneously appear to have failed, and yet not have done so. It must just survive, always, in spite of any possible argument and demonstration to the contrary.

May I state that once more in other terms?

Any truly Divine scheme — any scheme, that is to say, that is not human and finite — must always overlap any human criterion that can be applied to it. It must, that is, judged by purely human standards, be an apparent failure. But it must never be such a failure that it ceases to exist. You must be able to say of it, It has failed intellectually and emotionally; it does not correspond with the demand. And yet it survives. That is, it has not really failed at all.

Now it is a very significant fact that even human love, as we know it, must express itself in pain; that is to say, that the highest human happiness must express itself in terms of the deepest human misery. No human lover, in the real sense, can possibly describe love as being unmixed sweetness. Such words as "fever," and "smart," and "arrows" are always associated with love — in fact, they describe its very essence. The reason is not far to seek. Real love seeks not to possess, but to be possessed; not, so to speak, to devour the beloved, to satisfy self with the beloved, but the exact contrary — to be devoured and to satisfy. (That is why the Love of God, naturally greater than human love, insists upon the Sacrament of the altar.) Real love, then, is a continual emptying and slaying of self, a continual immolation of self on the altar of the beloved. This is simply a commonplace of human experience, described by every poet and artist since the world began. It is exactly this that distinguishes it from its caricature — its antichrist — from lust or liking. Lust and liking desire to acquire and to win; love to be acquired and to be won.

Now look at our two points together, and see how the Christian hypothesis exactly fits and explains the record of the Gospel. It is a record of Love expressing itself in Pain. Here is One who yearns for sacrifice — not on behalf of merely this or that person — but for all persons. " How am I straitened," cries Jesus Christ. " How am I compressed and confined, until this be accomplised! How am I held back and restrained until I am set at liberty by the fettering nails of the Cross — until I can empty myself wholly and entirely of every drop of blood, of every spiritual consolation — until I am indeed, in my Humanity, so utterly dry and wrung out that indeed I may be said to thirst — until I am so utterly lonely, in so appalling a solitude, that I have bidden even my mother farewell, have been forsaken of all my friends, and have lost even the perception of my Father's love. I am not truly possessed by my friends, until I have ceased to possess them." In one sentence, Christ could not be said to have succeeded in His object, until He had, down to the very least detail of His plan, completely failed. With Him, and Him alone, nothing succeeds like Failure.

Now, this identity of what the world calls failure and what God calls success is illustrated by many of Christ's deeper sayings, and lies luminous in the very heart of the darkness of Calvary. It is this surely that reconciles ultimately such paradoxes as —" Except a man lose his life, he cannot save it." " Blessed are they that hunger and thirst, for they shall be filled." " Blessed are they that mourn, for they shall be comforted." " Except a man hate not his father and mother, he cannot be My disciple," and " Except a man take up his cross "— reach, that is, the very lowest disgrace and failure that this world can conceive —" he cannot be My disciple." It seems, as we regard it, almost painfully obvious that, as I said just now, Divine Love cannot be said to have won any victory — cannot, that is, have fully expressed its own nature of Sacrifice, until it has undergone what the world reckons failure in every point. For Love must have pain,— more, it must become Pain — or else it dies indeed. Here, too, is the reconciliation of that most mysterious saying of all —

"He that believeth in Me shall never die,"— that is, "He that is really united with Me, finds Death to be the ultimate satisfaction of Love — and this is Life."

2. As we turn, then, from the record of Christ's Life in the Gospel to his Life in the Church, we find precisely the same phenomenon repeated over and over again.

Here is St. Paul first, crying in an ecstasy of Love —"I die daily "; "As dying, yet behold we live "; "I live, yet not I, but Christ liveth in me "; and above all, that phrase so often quoted before —"I fill up . . . what is lacking of the sufferings of Christ."

As we regard the Church, then, as the Body in which Jesus Christ leads a mystical life, a thousand difficulties are explained : —

1. First, What is that strange passion, which we have already considered in the chapter on Gethsemane, known only among Catholics as a wholesome and recognized instinct, by which men and women — even boys and girls — in the very height of vitality and strength, think that the one thing worth doing is to immure themselves in a cell, in order to suffer? What is the instinct that makes the Carmelite hang an empty cross in her cell, to remind herself that she must take the place of the absent figure upon it — and yet keeps the Carmelite the

most radiantly happy of all women. The joy of a woman — I might say the gayety of a woman — over her first child is but a shadow of the solemn joy of a Carmelite, the irrepressible gayety of a Poor Clare — women, that is, who have sacrificed every single thing that the world thinks worth having. Certainly it is not the same as Oriental asceticism, for the object of the Oriental is to escape from being, to be released from the Wheel of Life — and the object of the Catholic ascetic is to be bound to it more closely, to realize and express himself more fully — at least that kind of self-expression that is called self-sacrifice.

The thing is simply inexplicable except on one hypothesis — that that unique thirst of Jesus upon the Cross is communicated to His members, that His ambition to suffer is perpetuated continually in that Mystical Body in which He reënacts the history of His Passion — that these are the cells of that Body, which, like His Hands and Feet, are more especially pierced by nails, and who rejoice to know that they are called to this august vocation, by which the Redemption wrought on Calvary is perpetually reënacted on earth; who " fill up what is lacking of the sufferings of Christ," who are lambs of God whose blood mingles with the Blood on Calvary, victims whose sacrifice is accepted as united with His.

2. Again, as has been hinted before — this conception of the Church as the Body of Christ is surely the one hypothesis which makes the sufferings of *individuals* tolerable to contemplate. I have attempted to indicate how, as it appears to me, the problem of suffering in general will be ultimately solved — by arguing that Pain always is the expression of Love, that it is only an evil to those who do not love, and that it is a positive joy to those who, by love, accept and welcome it; and that Failure, as the world calls it, again and again corresponds to the necessary overlapping of the human by the Divine. But all this does not touch really the suffering of the individual who has not learnt how to welcome it. There still remains the problem of the little crippled child, and of the innocent girl who goes mad with melancholia.

Now if you treat those cases as individual — if you regard the child as merely a complete entity in himself, the thing is and always must be inexplicable. Again and again we find ourselves asking, why should *he* suffer? He is not a Carmelite who understands; he is not a sinner to be reformed by discipline.

But if you reflect that Humanity as a whole is a great organism, used by God as the Body of His passion: and that in the sufferings of this Body He carries out, on the mystical plane, His Redemption, and satisfies His Divine thirst for pain; and that this child is one cell of the Body of pain; you are no more intellectually puzzled as to why this child should suffer in particular, than you are intellectually puzzled as to why your finger should ache, instead of yourself. Your finger does not ache instead of yourself: you ache in your finger. This child does not suffer instead of Humanity; but Humanity suffers in him, and Christ therefore in him. If, in short, you will insist upon treating each unit only as a unit (which is, in a word, Protestantism)— you will never be satisfied; but if you understand that these units are more than units — they are cells in a Body; and if, further, you understand that it is Jesus Christ who lives and acts in this Body, that He truly, therefore, identifies Himself with every one of His members, a host of difficulties become luminous. " Inasmuch as ye do it, or do it not, unto one of the least of these — you do it, or do it not, to Me."

We have seen then, with a good many parentheses, that Pain and Failure must always be elements in the life of the Church. It must be possible for the world at any given moment to point to the Church and say, See what a failure! There must be a sense in which, judged by what is called " modern thought "— that is, human opinions and standards current at any given moment — the Church is condemned and crucified — hung, that is, between earth and heaven as one that is unworthy either to live or to die — as one that has failed to raise earth to heaven, or to bring heaven down to earth.

There must be a sense, in fact, in which the Church must not only be a failing cause, but a cause that has actually failed — a cause that is both dead and buried. It must continually, according to these standards, be completely discredited, as one who has promised to accomplish much, but has accomplised nothing; one who has claimed to be King, but has only earned a mock crown of thorns; one who has professed to save others, but cannot save even himself.

Again and again that taunt must go up, " Come down from the Cross and we will believe. . . . Relinquish that failure, and make it a success. Cease to claim to be Divine — for you see how hopelessly you fail to justify it. See what happens to one who makes Himself Divine — and be human instead. Come down to our level, and be a man among men; and we will believe, and accept you as at least our Master."

But that taunt cannot be accepted. The failure must be entire. The last spark of life must die out, obedient unto death — that one irremediable disaster. "And Jesus cried with a loud voice, It is finished; and He bowed His head and gave up the ghost."

Finally, the Body must be laid in a tomb, and a stone rolled over it. "Christianity is a lost cause at last," must be the comment of what are called "all thinking men"; . . . and even His lovers must begin to despair. "We thought that it had been He who should have redeemed Israel, and now . . . !"

II

The comment of every age pronounced against the Catholic Church is that she has failed (it is said) in every work to which she has set her hand, and from every point of view from which the world regards her. She is not political enough for Caiphas, but she is too political for Pilate; she is not sensational enough for Herod; she is too sensational for the Pharisees. She is too ugly for the Greeks; she is too beautiful for the Puritans. She is too dogmatic for the modern religious mystics; she is too mystical for the modern scientific dogmatists. She has either over-emphasized or under-emphasized every element of truth which the world acknowledges her to possess. She is too ascetic in her teaching of celibacy; she is too imprudent and unphilosophical in her teaching on the married life; she is too leisurely and contemplative for the philanthropists; she is too active and zealous for the spiritually-minded. She is too rationalistic and precise in her theology for the sentimental; she is too senti-

mental for the rationalists.   She is too hard on the
heretics; she is too easy towards the sinners.

Listen to the comments of the world upon her in
the earliest ages.   " Look at this terrible people,"
writes Pliny, in effect, " called Christians — a mo-
rose, depressed, miserable race of men who hate the
sunlight; gloomy, dark and superstitious."   " Look
at the shocking gayety of these martyrs," complain
the magistrates —" Laurence jesting on his grid-
iron; girls and children smiling to meet the embrace
of the panther."   Listen to the same comments of
the same world at the present day.   " Look at the
morbid, pain-loving superstition of these Catholics,
with their fastings and scourgings and asceticism.
And look at the un-Christian gayety of the Conti-
nental Sunday."   " We have piped unto you," said
Jesus Christ, " and you have not danced: we have
mourned unto you and you have not lamented."
We are all like children playing in the market-place.
We have asked you to play at weddings — we have
preached the joy of life — and you have refused:
we have asked you to play at funerals — we have
preached the sorrow of life — and you have refused.
We have given you happy and contented monks,
for example, and you have mocked and caricatured
them in your comic papers.   We have given you
sorrowful ascetics, and you have said that long
faces were not a good advertisement for any re-

ligion. " In fact," cries the world, " you are too extreme in every direction at once. You are too happy and too miserable, too keen and too contented, too mystical and too dogmatic, too objective and too subjective. You have had your chance, and you have failed to convert us: you have been weighed in the balances and found wanting."

Let us look at it all from another angle.

At certain great periods in history there come those moments at which what is called, at each such moment, " modern thought " is apparently victorious.

In one century it took the form of Orientalism and the rise of the Gnostics — when there swept over large districts of Christendom schemes of belief that threatened altogether to overwhelm Catholicism. It seemed to observer after observer that the Faith of the Gospels was submerged — never to rise again. In another century it was Arianism: " the world groaned to find itself Arian " — the great defenders of the Nicene Faith vanished in exile, discredited and silenced. In another period it was the power of the Turk, who captured Jerusalem, regained Africa, and even established itself in Spain. At another time it was worldliness in the Church itself. The Popes disappeared from Rome; there seemed not one prophet any more, nor one that understood. The old gods came back;

Paganism reasserted itself; the simplicity and the purity of the Gospel vanished in a storm of revelry. Then this enemy disappeared, to be succeeded by one far more dangerous and subtle, when the world rose up against the Church, actually in the name of God Himself, claiming to purify and restore that original truth which the Church had deformed and ruined.

Let us consider that a little more in detail.

It is almost impossible in these days to realize the immensity and the success of that movement known as the Reformation. Europe consisted more or less of two great divisions — the southerners and the northerners; and there was no question that the virility of the continent, and its hope for the future, lay with the Saxons and the Teutons rather than with the Latins. Take England and Spain as representatives of the two. Spain was indeed a vast power in the world, wealthy beyond imagination, proud, aristocratic and overbearing — yet it was the strength of maturity rather than of youth. England stood for adolescence and the future, rather than for maturity and the past. And it was at this moment of all others, when the Church was weakened by the Renaissance and assaulted by the " New Learning," that the younger and more vigorous nations of the world declared against her with one consent. That movement, which arose in Germany, spread to England, and, with the pilgrims to the

New World, to America itself; and it must have
seemed to every student of history that, if anything
could be predicted as absolutely certain, it was that
it could only be a matter of a very few years before
the Latin nations finally crumbled away, and with
them the prestige and influence of that Church
which had ruled in them so long.   Every precedent
that history could show was against the Church.
Every empire that the world had ever seen had
gone through precisely the same stages down to
death — from the vigor and purity of youth, through
the experience of maturity, down to the dissolution
of old age.   Each empire in turn had exhibited
exactly the same symptoms, sharing always in its
last stages that same kind of corrupt exuberance
as the Church showed in the Renaissance.   Was it
any wonder, then, that Saxon and Teutonic Protestantism declared that the hour of God had struck
at last, and that the Power which had ruled so long
— which had succeeded to the domination of Imperial Rome — had finally and ultimately run its
course, and that the Church of Rome was dead at
last?

Now, this was precisely what was actually said
again and again by the preachers of the New Religion.   John Bunyan said it, in his classification
of Pope and Pagan as the two discredited powers
that still barked but could no longer bite: John

Milton said it again and again. The judges and divines who taunted the captured seminary priests in England said it. Their whole attitude towards the supporters of the old Faith was one of contempt, rather than of fear. It was so obvious, as they looked round England, that the cause of Rome was dead and buried. There, all about them, lay the ruins of the Religious Houses and the monasteries; there in the quadrangles of Oxford blew about the pages of those old Catholic books of learning, discredited and found out at last: the mercers of Malvern corded their wares in them; grocers used them for the wrapping up of sugar and salt. Even the old vestments were gone, fashioned into stomachers and bedquilts for the wives of the new and enlightened clergy; the altar-stones paved the aisles of the churches in which they had been reverenced so long; the shrines were down — the images were burned; and, with the exception of a few fanatics in the north and west, the whole country acquiesced in the change.

From over the seas came the same story. Everywhere, as the New Religion spread on the lips of preachers and the pages of new printed books, district after district caught fire. It seemed as if all the powers of the world fought in their courses against the priestly tyranny that had prevailed so long. It was the ships of the Protestants that fought best; the armies of the Protestants that were the more fervent and the more effective; the very printing-press itself, with its new and undreamed-of power of disseminating knowledge, seemed on the side of the new Faith and not of the old. Finally, the new energy of colonization was all on the Protestant side. If there was anything absolutely certain to those who knew what history and precedent meant, who understood the great laws of rise and fall, and energy and maturity and death, it was that since — as they said — Papal Rome was one of those great world-powers, like the empires of Persia or Assyria, like Greece and Imperial Rome, it must undergo the inevitable fate of all those world-powers, and pass away into dissolution. They went even further than that; they said that it had already happened, that Rome was gone as a world-power; that she reigned only as a ghost might reign over a sepulcher, where its body lay. They said that all her real influence was dead; that she had once ruled the courts of Kings, but that she no longer ruled them; that she had once controlled the destinies of Europe, but that she no longer controlled them; that she was already dead and buried; that the stone was on her tomb; and that the secular powers must see to it that that stone was not removed; in short, that she who had professed to save others, could not even save herself; that she failed wholly and entirely to justify her enormous claims; that she was an impostor found out at last.

We hear echoes of all this even at the present day.

"We have extinguished," said Viviani in France the other day, "with a magnificent gesture, and altogether, the lights that have burned in heaven so long." Mr. Joseph McCabe, an apostate Franciscan friar, has lately published an enormous book to prove that the Church of Rome is dead. The Rev. Alfred Fawkes, ex-Anglican, ex-Oratorian, and finally ex-priest and Anglican once again, in a picturesque little essay, compares the Papacy to an iceberg, whose disappearance is certain under the rays of the Sun of Modern Truth which has recently dawned. In practically every secular newspaper that is published, and in a good many religious newspapers as well, the same assertion is made again and again. We are told by some that National Churches are the only solution of the religious question; by others, that it lies only in congregational groups or societies, without any particular creeds or articles of faith; by others again — for instance the Modernists — that the modern religion must be completely unlike the old, that the old dogmas will no longer hold water, that the old idea that religion could be defined by an authority,

and tested by references to a positive body of revelation, can no longer possibly be held by " thinking
men."   But, in whatever direction the solution may
be thought to lie, it is assumed, almost as an axiom,
that the Church of Rome is a completely dead and
discredited body, that her day is over at last, and
that there are left to weep round her tomb but a
few feeble-minded or heartbroken mourners, to
whom even the dead body of a religion that is past
is more dear than all the promises and aspirations
of a world that looks now in another direction for
light and leading.

" And Joseph taking the body, wrapped it up in
a new clean linen cloth.   And laid it in his own new
monument which he had hewn out in a rock.   And
he rolled a great stone to the door of the monument
and went his way.   And there were there Mary
Magdalene and the other Mary, sitting over against
the sepulcher. .   .   .

" And (the chief priests and the Pharisees) de-
parting, made the sepulcher sure, sealing the stone,
and setting guards." [1]

[1] Matt. xxvii. 59–61, and 66.

III

We considered in the last chapter how once more in our day modern religious thought has pronounced the cause of Catholicism practically extinct; and how many of those thinkers who are thought to be in the forefront of progress no longer consider that the Church is even an enemy to be met. Yet it is remarkable that these philosophers do not seem to reflect that the dirge has been sung over the grave of the Church of Rome not less than ten or twelve times already, in almost universal chorus, in the history of the past, and that every single time it has somehow died away — that the same things have been said again and again and again, and that each time all predictions have been completely falsified. Nero said it; Arius said it; Henry VIII said it; Voltaire said it; and now Viviani, Mr. McCabe and Mr. Fawkes take up the chant with undiminished confidence. And yet, somehow or another, the Body lives. Oh! I acknowledge freely that it ought to have died; that it is clean against all precedent and all experience; that Nero's persecution ought to have stamped it out, but that somehow it did not; that Arius' arguments were amazingly common-sense and ought to have silenced the Catholic paradox that Jesus was both God and Man, but that somehow they did not; that Sabellius' argument, that if God were really one, He could not be really three, ought to have convinced all persons who think themselves "thinking men," but that somehow it did not; that Henry VIII and Elizabeth were really brilliant politicians and administrators, and that their policy in destroying the religious houses and insulting the most sacred shrines of England ought to have put an end forever to what they called "Popish superstition," but that somehow it did not; that McCabe's statistics are admirably worked out, and demonstrate practically that there is no such thing as the Church of Rome at all — and yet that somehow there is; that Viviani's measures are extremely forcible, and ought to have finished the affair five years ago — only somehow the affair is not finished; that the Modernists, supported as they are by such ecclesiastical authorities as the *Times* newspaper, to which they appeal, ought to have said the last word, but that somehow the Pope still issues Encyclicals; in short, that if the Catholic Church were what these people suppose it to be, an extremely well-organized human society, like any other earthly kingdom or association, it certainly would have perished, if not under Nero, at any rate under Napoleon; that if its articles of belief were just the result of extremely clever and subtle human theorizing, they ought to have been extinguished, if not by Arius and Sabellius, at least by Voltaire — or, at any rate, modified by the Abbé Loisy or Mr. Fawkes.

I said just now that it was remarkable that these philosophers and historians and sociologists do not seem to be aware that their predictions have been already uttered and falsified at least ten or twelve times before in the history of Catholicism. But it seems to me even more remarkable that they are choosing this particular moment, of all others, to repeat them. Fifty years ago, or a hundred years ago, there might have been some shadow of excuse; at the time of the Reformation there was a great deal of excuse; in the heart of the Renaissance, or the captivity of Avignon, even more. Even forty years ago when Rome fell and the Pope fled, it might have appeared quite reasonable to have declared that the blow had fallen at last — as indeed it was declared — and that historical precedent was justified; but now! . . . now of all moments!

Now I am aware that statistics — the mere counting of heads, that is to say — can be manipulated so as to prove almost anything (Mr. McCabe shows us that); and I do not propose to compete with him.   Since, however, it is seriously maintained by apparently reasonable people that the Church of Rome is dying, if not dead, it is, I suppose, necessary to do something to show my own conviction that, so far from this being the fact, we are on the very verge — as Mr. H. G. Wells tells us — of a revival of Catholicism, in the world as a whole, such as the world has never yet seen; that the religion of the immediate future, at any rate — at least such religion as there is — will not take the form of diluted Protestantism, or of a system of ethics or Modernism, or of a kind of pious Pantheism (which is about what the newly discovered doctrine of Immanence amounts to — though Immanence and its correlative Transcendence have in a sense been preached by the Catholic Church from the first moment of her existence); that the religion of the future will be none of these, but dogmatic, credal, disciplinary and Papal Catholicism, such as has been known from the beginning.

1. First, then, there has never been a time when Devotion — and devotion in its most practical form, and directed to an object which the world considers the very acme of Catholic foolishness — I mean the Sacrament of the Altar — has been so intense. Those who were present in London a couple of years ago at the Eucharistic Congress must surely have been aware of this fact.   Not only were the streets

nearly impassable with a crowd beyond all reckoning, gathered from every country of Europe, but even the solemn British Constitution itself was troubled. Certainly other societies could have embarrassed the politicians, and blocked Victoria Street; but I am sure that no society in the world could have aroused such intense feeling of love and adoration on one side, and of fury and terror on the other, with regard to a small white object which one-half of that world declared to be a piece of Bread. I do not in the least wish to avoid discussion on this point which is the very heart of Catholic devotion; but this is not the occasion on which to discuss it in full. But I will only draw attention for an instant to this matter — that the Eucharistic Congress of London in 1908 — and the Eucharistic Congress of Cologne in 1909, with the Papal delegate sailing up the Rhine to the roar of cannon and the pealing of bells — that the Eucharistic Congress of this year at Montreal, are all gathered, not to dispute as to the question, or to argue about modes in which it is to be interpreted, but simply to do honor and glory to the Fact (as Catholics believe it) that Jesus Christ, God and Man, takes Bread and makes it His Body, and that the Human Nature, born of Mary, crucified on Calvary, and raised on Easter Day 2,000 years ago, is present to-day under the appearance of bread, in London, in Cologne and Montreal, and in every Catholic tabernacle in every Catholic church throughout the world. I am not discussing whether it is true or not; I am only attempting to show that a period which produces such phenomena as these Congresses, which gathers those international and supranational multitudes together for the glorifying of this central dogma, is scarcely the period to select for the assertion of Rome's decay. And if the doctrine appears to those philosophers — as it does — ludicrous and silly, the phenomena is the more inexplicable. It is impossible to dismiss these crowds of worshipers as mere barbarians and savages, mad with fanaticism; for there worshiped amongst them, scientists, doctors, philosophers, astronomers, judges on the bench, lawyers at the bar, soldiers, business-men, merchants, as well as women and children — those who with natural purity of heart, naturally see God.

2. Secondly, it is probably true to say that seldom, if ever, have the wise and prudent of the world shown themselves more willing to accept Catholicism when once it has been presented to them. I have already touched on this point, and need not dwell on it now at any length. Recent conversions in France, as well as in England, have surely put it beyond the power of any critic to say that the Church appeals merely to the uneducated. It is

perfectly true to say that many of the wise and
prudent to whom the Church is presented reject
her; and that the fact that others accept her is not
a proof that she is what she claims to be. But the
fact that some do accept her — some of those, that
is, who are aware of all that can be said against
her, who know perfectly well the arguments of
science and biology and all the rest — this, at any
rate, is a proof that she is not *contrary* to those
things. Father Cortie, the Jesuit astronomer, is
quite aware of the fact that the earth is but one
of the planets, yet he finds no difficulty in believing
that the Son of God was incarnate on the earth.
Professor Windle — a recent convert — is fully
acquainted with all that has ever been said or sur-
mised as to the constitution of matter, and yet he
has deliberately chosen to believe that the substance
of Bread is changed at five words uttered by a
priest, into the substance of the Body of Jesus
Christ. Lord Brampton was as well aware of the
insufficiency of human evidence as any man who
has ever lived, and yet he, too, in the very height
of his powers and his reputation, chose to become
as a little child, and to believe and to do as he was
told by other human beings far less accomplished
than himself. The Professor of History at Halle
University knows all that can be said as to the
secular causes and circumstances that are urged as

the reason of Rome's preëminence, and yet the other day he made himself a student at her feet, and accepted as his Mistress and Queen her whom he had been taught to criticize and reject. Is this period, marked by the conversion of men of this kind, in every civilized country of the world, the time to say that the Church of Rome is evidently false, that her claims are at least disproved, and that no " thinking man " can possibly ever look for enlightenment in her direction?

3. A third sign of her undying vitality lies in the attitude of so many of those towards her who have no ax to sharpen, either against her, or in her quarrel — I mean that attitude expressed by those who say, " I do not profess to have any religion; but if I were a religious man at all, I would be a Catholic."

Now this sounds a very slight matter; but the thing is so common, at least in my experience — (I have had it said to me by total strangers again and again, in the street, in railway trains, and on the tops of omnibuses)— that it must stand for something rather significant. If you press the man who says this a little further, he will generally say, " Well, you Catholics at any rate know your own minds; and you do what you're told. You're all the same, everywhere; you haven't got one religion for one man and another for another."

15

Sum that up in a sentence. It is this. The man somehow or another has knocked up against this very vitality of which I am speaking. He has discovered — Heaven only knows how — that the Church is a living organism, very much alive; that she has a mind of her own; that she is not just a code, but a being, which thinks and speaks; not just a collection of individuals who agree to call themselves by one name, but are agreed hardly on anything else; that she is not an antique survival, or an æsthetic club, or a loosely knit human society of any kind whatever, but a vital and imperious Person, who speaks, moves and acts as a person should. He has discovered, in short, that very thing of which I have spoken again and again, that she is quite unlike any other society in the whole world. He sets her by herself, and the rest all together, and says, "If I were anything, I would be a Catholic."

Once more, then, is this the time to speak of the decay of the Church of Rome; when not only the disciples, but the very stones cry out — those very souls who lie beneath her, motionless and inert, and yet have wit enough to recognize the thrill and vibration of her feet? If the Church were dead and discredited, would these things be said of her?

4. Fourthly, I would like to recall another point I have already discussed at length — the manner in which one by one her ancient conclusions, at least

in the realm of phenomena, are being painfully veri- fied by science.

We live in the days of psychology. All sciences, more and more, are finding that in psychology lies an immense amount of evidence necessary for their own perfection. Biology is coming to its center, which is consciousness: History is discovering that events must be interpreted according to the characters of those who witness to those events, that character is complicated after all, and not simple, and that therefore events are complicated, too: Medicine is discovering that the attitude of mind of a patient is at least as much an element in his cure as are the things administered to him. There has sprung up, then, a school of psychology that hopes some day to supply the central key to all these mysteries; and the very first fact that psychology has stumbled upon is this — that religion in general supplies what is probably the strongest secret, as well as open, motive of the human mind, and that the Catholic religion in particular, which has witnessed alone continuously and unwaveringly to this central fact, also supplies the greatest wealth of extraordinary and significant phenomena produced by it. All these ancient truths, known to Catholicism from the days of Jesus Christ downwards — the healing power of faith, the abnormal states of body produced by an interior condition, communications at a distance, apparitions of the dead, the possibilities of what are apparently two characters in one organism — all these things maintained by Catholicism, and hitherto denied scornfully by science, are found to be objective facts after all, and must be dealt with in some way before any real progress can be made. Is this the time, then, to speak of the Death of the Catholic Church, when she has just been discovered, even by psychologists, to be so appallingly alive, and to possess powers — powers of suggestion and stimulus, if you prefer to call them so — which no other body, up to recent times, has claimed or even confessed to exist?

It would be possible, I think, to continue almost indefinitely with these signs of undying vitality. It would be possible to show that the stability of all Society, the one safeguard against anarchism, the one protector of domestic life, the one inspirer of art, the one competent adversary of race-suicide, has lain in the past and will lie in the future, in the Catholic Church and the Catholic Church only. After all, she alone has been able to preserve from the past what is best worth preserving; it was she who saved the music of the old world from total destruction, who transformed and preserved the architecture of that same world, as well as invented a new one of her own on which practically all future progress must depend; it is she who has saved the life of Latin and Greek, using them with her lips as well as in printed books of the past; it is she who has caught up philosophy after philosophy and made them the vehicles of her own truth; it is she, in short, who has been the mother of all civilization as we know it; and it is where she has been rejected and thrust aside that that civilization is already beginning to crumble. Compare the art-galleries of the Luxembourg and the Louvre, the one pagan, the other Christian, and ask yourselves honestly, which is the finer art of the two? Or put the ideas of Fraternity, Liberty, and Equality, as understood in France now, beside those same qualities as understood in the ages of chivalry, and ask yourselves which promise best for the stability of Society. Or look even at Anglo-Saxon countries and honestly decide where lies the best hope of continuance — in that Society which is believed to consist in a race for wealth or reputation among units each fighting for his own hand, each following his own heart and his own private judgment (which is the very essence of Protestantism) both in America and England — or in a Society where there may indeed be tyranny from time to time, and abuse of power, and undue cringing, but where at any rate the theory is that the Christian Society is a mystical Body in which Christ dwells, in which each member has his vocation, his duties and his responsibilities, and an eternal future in which the performance of those duties will find its right reward.

All this, however, is too vast and complicated for our purposes.   Only, I have no fear of the result if the question is but honestly faced and honestly answered.

This, then, in a word, is my final argument — and it is that to which Christ Himself ultimately appealed — the argument of Resurrection, for nothing can raise itself from death, except Divinity. We have seen a number of points in which the Life of the Catholic Church corresponds strangely and wonderfully with the Life of Christ.

We have seen the characteristics of those who accept and those who reject the claims that the Church makes; those who accept — the simple on the one side and the highly educated on the other; those who reject — the middle kind of intellect which has not learned enough to know the limitations of knowledge; and we saw how these classes corresponded with those who respectively accepted and rejected Jesus Christ.   Then, after touching on the element of hiddenness and contemplation which mark alike the Life in the Gospels and the Life in the Church, and seeing how that witnessed to a consciousness of something beyond the things of sense, we considered the substance, mode, and sanctions of the teaching of the Gospels and the Church. The substance in four points was the same, and those points of a very startling character, productive of the same kind of protest in all ages from those who reject them. And the manner of the teaching is the same — an authoritativeness and finality that can only rise from a consciousness of the possession of absolute Truth — an authoritativeness that must always be a mark of such consciousness. Then we discussed the miraculous element in both alike, and noticed how a Teacher who claims to be Divine must exhibit these signs, and that a world that rejects the Teacher must explain them away, as the critics of Jesus Christ explained them then, and as the critics of Catholicism explain them now. Then we passed on more particularly to the kind of characters that reject Divine Teaching in all ages — Caiphas, the representative of all religious societies that are simply human; Pilate, the type of all who think that Truth must be a rare and elusive thing; and Herod, for whom Truth consists in the abnormal and sensational. Then summing all this up we saw how the three great divisions of worldly energy — the supporters of Law, the pursuers of subjective Truth, and the lovers of the Beautiful,— however various their ideals, yet all unite in condemning Him who claims to be the Way, the Truth, and the Life; and that these same thinkers to-day, disunited in all else, are united in this alone — that they condemn and reject Catholicism as the one common enemy of them all. Finally, we considered the failure of both Christ and His Church; and attempted to see whether the ultimate tragedy of Calvary in all ages was not, as a matter of fact, the one condition of all success considered from the Divine standpoint — whether Love must not express itself in pain, and Christ be dead and buried before He could conquer the supreme enemies of man. That the Church has always failed is perfectly evident to every student of history; she has failed in a degree in which no human society has ever failed without extinction. She has passed through, again and again, in country after country, at the hands of heretics, persecutors, critics, philosophers, and worldly powers and energies of every description, every phase of failure and condemnation which it is possible to imagine. She has not succeeded in satisfying perfectly any single human instinct; she has always broken down under (as her enemies would say), or transcended (as her friends say), every demand made upon her. No one except her own prejudiced friends is satisfied with her, it seems; no one finds in her that degree of humanity which he desires. She is always echoing the cry of the world —" I thirst " with the same cry on her own lips; she is always discredited, always found out, always dying, always forsaken by God and man, even down to death itself; she is always being buried; she is always vanishing under stone and seal, always being classed by the world with every other form and system of belief that has passed or is passing into the grave.

And yet she lives.

Once more we saw that that which in every age calls itself "Modern Thought" has, once more in our own, pronounced sentence of death upon her — has done more, has declared life actually extinct. And, simultaneously, we see that she lives with an impulse and vitality that are simply unique in human history; that, at the very moment when the "wise and prudent" declare her dead, the wise and the prudent turn to her as the source of all life and knowledge; that at the very moment when the masses are alienated from her, the masses turn to her once again as their Mother and Queen; that there has never been a period when her devotion has been more fervent, her discipline more perfect, and her hopes higher. Even three hundred years — so short a time in her history who has lived from the beginning and will live to the end! — have seen the rise and fall of countless sects; but never hers. Nationalism has crumbled into Congregationalism; Congregationalism into Individualism; and Individualism has once again begun to cohere under new and fantastic forms; but she remains exactly as she was.

Other religious societies have found it necessary to issue new dogmas and new conceptions, to recast thought as Arius did, or Sabellius, or Voltaire, or the Abbé Loisy; she alone retains the old; and, simultaneously, where the new religions crumble, in spite of their professed adaptability to the times, she remains rigid, and yet retains more countries under her sway, and more temperaments among her lovers, than all the new religions have ever dreamed of.

I do not for one instant profess to believe that all the world is about to turn Catholic: I am quite sure that it is not; I even think it probable that we are on the verge of a Great Apostasy; but of one point I am as certain as of my own existence, that fifty years hence there will be no considerable body in the whole of western Christendom which will be able for one moment to compete with her; and that a thousand years hence, if the world lasts so long, we shall have once more the same situation that we have now.

On the one side will stand human society ranged against her, in ranks and companies of which hardly two members are agreed upon anything except upon opposition to her. There will be the New Theologians of that day, as of ours; new schools of thought, changing every instant, new discoveries, new reve-

lations, new presentations and combinations of frag-
ments of old truth. And on the other side will stand
the Church of the ages, with the marks of her
Passion deeper than ever upon her. From the one
side will go up that all but eternal cry, " We have
found her out at last; she is forsaken of all except
of a few fanatics at last; she is dead and buried at
last." And on the other side she will stand, then
as always, wounded indeed to death, yet not dead;
betrayed by her new-born Judases, judged by her
Herods and her Pilates, scourged by those who pity
while they strike, despised and rejected, and yet
stronger in her Divine foolishness than all the wisdom of men; hung between Heaven and earth, and
yet victorious over both; sealed and guarded in her
living tomb, and yet always and forever passing
out to new life and new victories.

So, too, then as now, and as at the beginning,
there will be secret gardens where she is known and
loved, where she will console the penitent as the sun
rises on Easter Day; there will be upper rooms
where her weeping friends are gathered for fear of
the Jews, when, the doors being shut, she will come
and stand in the midst and give them Peace; on
mountains, and roads, and by the sea, she will walk
then, as she has walked always, in the secret splen-
dor of her Resurrection. So once more the wheel
will turn; there will be ten thousand Bethlehems

where she is born again and again; the kings of the earth will bring their glory and honor to lay at her feet, side by side with the shepherds who have no gifts but themselves to offer.   Again and again that old and eternal story will be told and retold as each new civilization comes into being and passes away — that old drama reënacted wherever the Love of God confronts the needs of men.   She has already seen the rise and fall of dynasty after dynasty, of monarchies and republics; she will see in the future, no doubt, Socialism on the one side — that tyranny of Society over the individual, and Anarchy on the other — that tyranny of the individual over Society.   She has seen so far all the conceivable theories of life rise and die away, and she, the Life, remains the same.   She has seen a thousand schools of thought and aspects of Truth; and she, the Truth, remains the same.   She has seen all these, and she will see many more; but she will see them all to bed before the end comes — before that Mystical Body of Christ, which she is, has attained that measure of the stature of the fullness of Christ which is her eternal destiny and her certain hope.   For this is her final and supreme appeal — that sign of the Prophet Jonas — that miracle of Resurrection to which she has always appealed, and which has never failed her yet.

It is possible, as we have seen, for those who are

determined to do so, to explain away her miracles;
it is possible to make out excellent reasons for her
success in uniting those whom nationality divided;
it is possible to account for her sanctity by psychological arguments upon temperaments and the power
of suggestion; it is possible to meet her philosophy
with another philosophy, her statistics by other statistics, and her arguments by answers.   But is it
possible to meet the phenomenon of her agelong
Resurrection by any explanation that will not break
down — to account, on secular or social principles,
for the fact that while she has met reverses which
no other religion or empire or society has ever been
called upon to meet, yet she is more vital than them
all?   That she is as young and as active as she was
a thousand years ago, as much an obstacle to all
worldly politicians, as much an offense to all who
seek another ideal than hers, as much a scandal
and a stumbling-block to her critics, as she was
when Nero ruled or Elizabeth tyrannized or Arius
or Voltaire sneered.

*For I see through her eyes, the Eyes of God to
shine, and through her lips I hear His words.   In
each of her hands as she raises them to bless, I see
the wounds that dripped on Calvary, and her feet
upon her Altar stairs are signed with the same
marks as those which the Magdalene kissed.   As
she comforts me in the confessional I hear the voice*

that bade the sinner go and sin no more; and as she rebukes or pierces me with blame I shrink aside trembling with those who went out one by one, beginning with the eldest, till Jesus and the penitent were left alone. As she cries her invitation through the world I hear the same ringing claim as that which called, " Come unto me and find rest to your souls"; as she drives those who profess to serve her from her service I see the same flame of wrath that scourged the changers of money from the temple courts.

As I watch her in the midst of her people, applauded by the mob shouting always for the rising sun, I see the palm branches about her head, and the City and Kingdom of God, it would seem, scarcely a stone's throw away, yet across the valley of the Kedron and the garden of Gethsemane; and as I watch her pelted with mud, spurned, spat at and disgraced, I read in her eyes the message that we should weep not for her but for ourselves and for our children, since she is immortal and we but mortal after all. As I look on her white body, dead and drained of blood, I smell once more the odor of the ointments and the trampled grass of that garden near to the place where He was crucified, and hear the tramp of the soldiers who came to seal the stone and set the watch. And, at last, as I see her moving once more in the dawn light of each new day, or in the revelation of evening, as the sun of this or that dynasty rises and sets, I understand that He who was dead has come forth once more with healing in His wings, to comfort those that mourn and to bind up the brokenhearted; and that His coming is not with observation, but in the depth of night as His enemies slept and His lovers woke for sorrow.

Yet even as I see this I understand that Easter is but Bethlehem once again; that the cycle runs round again to its beginning and that the conflict is all to fight again; for they will not be persuaded, though One rises daily from the dead.

THE END